THE WORKS MINIS

THE
WORKS MINIS

*An illustrated history of the Works entered
Minis in international rallies and races*

BY
PETER BROWNING

First published 1971

Reprinted 1974

Reprinted in paperback form 1979, 1982, 1984, 1986 & 1988

© Peter Browning 1971, 1979

ISBN 0 85429 278 0

A FOULIS Motoring Book

Published by
The Haynes Publishing Group
Sparkford, Nr Yeovil, Somerset BA22 7JJ
England

Haynes Publications Inc.
861 Lawrence Drive, Newbury Park
California 91320

ACKNOWLEDGEMENTS

The story of the Works Minis encompasses the experiences of a remarkable number of people. Had I been able to track them all down then this story could have filled many volumes; indeed one could almost write a book about every event in which the Abingdon Minis took part! It has not, therefore, been easy to determine the moment to call a halt to the never ending research work and get down to writing the Mini story.

I want to thank sincerely all who have contributed in any way to this story, though there is not space here to mention them all by name but I must record my gratitude for particular help from the following: Doug Watts told me a lot about the early days of the Competitions Department and Cliff Humphries helped me compile the chapter on Mini Mechanics. Paddy Hopkirk, Rauno Aaltonen and John Rhodes have provided the basis of the chapter on Mini Driving. I am also grateful to Jeremy Ferguson and Iain Mills of Dunlop for their help with the chapter on Mini Tyres. The British Leyland Photographic Department at Cowley provided nearly all of the pictures. Sandy Lawson helped me go through the old Abingdon records while Elizabeth Aves typed my final manuscripts.

Hendon, London   Peter Browning
July 1971

CONTENTS

ILLUSTRATIONS

CHAPTER 1

THE ABINGDON TOUCH

One of the fascinating things about international rallying is that
to win you do not always have to have the best car. Team spirit and
the will to win can make up for a lot. This is the story of a rally team
that, for quite a short time, did have the best car and with it won a
remarkable number of rallies. But rather more significant, the team
and the car went on winning for a longer period when that car was
not considered competitive. That team was the Competitions Department of the British Motor Corporation (later British Leyland) and
the car that will always be associated with their successes was the
Mini.

Before we trace the story of the works Minis in competition we
should take a look at the most significant aspect that contributed to
the team's success – the team spirit which could well be named 'the
Abingdon touch'.

From the days when Cecil Kimber had Morris Garages build his
first MG special, the little Abingdon factory has thrived in a motor
sporting atmosphere. With enthusiasts like John Thornley (Managing
Director) and Syd Enever (Chief Designer) around, Abingdon was
obviously the place to base the BMC Competitions Department when
it was formed in 1954. The Department was first established within
the MG Development shop under the command of Syd Enever.
There were three sections in the shop – MG development, customer
tuning and competitions. With Syd's main interest being racing and
record breaking and the building of the MGA prototypes, it was soon
clear that the Competitions side needed a manager and Marcus
Chambers was appointed to lead the team.

Marcus is a big jovial fellow who very early on earned the nickname
of 'Chub' and the 'Poor Man's Neubauer'. He came to Abingdon
with a vast knowledge of production cars in competition having
served as the chief racing mechanic to HRG and driven at Le Mans
in pre-war years. He was particularly astute when it came to sorting
out the rules and regulations of motor sport, a proficient linguist, a

much travelled man and, to the delight of his colleagues, a lover of good food and wine!

Marcus would be the first to acknowledge the significant part played by John Thornley in those early days. When it came to decisions on competition matters, John was a man with vast experience and foresight. He was a born leader and had a unique way of transmitting his enthusiasm to those who worked under him. While he appreciated that a Competitions Manager likes to be left alone to get on with running the show as he thinks fit, John was always on hand to give advice and fight the political battles with the higher management. This he did with the same forceful effect that he applied to his constant efforts to see that MGs were built as Abingdon wanted them built and not as Longbridge commanded. It was sad that his early retirement meant that he was not in command at Abingdon to help the Competitions Department fight its last and most important political battle.

Doug Watts–team leader

Someone who was involved with the Competitions Department right from its earlier days and the man who more than anyone inspired the team to winning form, was Doug Watts, the shop's first foreman and in later years its supervisor. Like practically everyone in the team, Doug is a Berkshireman, born and bred. His father was a local butcher and Doug's first job was as a clerk in the local brewery. Even at this early age his lifelong dislike of paperwork was apparent and he soon moved on to the carpenter's shop where he showed a remarkable aptitude with the tools of the trade. He later became a fitter in the metal shop and, after a few years, had done every job in the brewery including serving as a drayman.

In the war he served for a short period in the Territorials and then got a job at the MG factory which was then working on armoured cars and tanks. Although his work at Abingdon impressed his seniors, Doug left to join the Engineers and passed out as a top-grade fitter which gained him a posting to North Africa working on the railways. This led to a spell as an engine driver in Italy and undoubtedly keeping old trains on the move in difficult times nurtured the qualities of determination and improvisation that he was to display to such good effect in his later years at Abingdon. And yet at this time Doug openly declared his dislike of rank and class distinction for he constantly turned down promotion and, on one occasion, lost his 'stripe' for insubordination!

Returning to Abingdon post-war, Doug was welcomed back at MG where after a time as a rectification fitter on the MG TC line, he was promoted as one of three road test inspectors. This job well suited his skills and temperament for in those days the testers took the cars straight from the line, went out for a drive, found out what was wrong and put it right with their own bag of tools at the roadside. When the Riley Pathfinder was introduced, Doug was put in command of the 10,000-mile road test of the prototypes and was later sent out on a round-the-world trip to put right a design fault on the early production cars. This again was good grounding for the future for, when it was announced that the Competitions Department was to be formed, one reason that Doug got the job was that he was one of the few people at MG with a passport!

It was Alec Houslow, Development Department foreman, who picked Doug for the job and anyone who has had anything to do with the Competitions Department, will tell you that he could not have picked a better man. It was Doug who selected the mechanics and the foremen and he was a remarkable judge of a man's character and ability. It was he who established how the team should work together – something that was to prove so vital to moulding that all-important team spirit. Above all, he was able to transmit his unbounded energy, enthusiasm and loyalty to those around him.

The Team is formed

In its earlier days the team comprised a selection of the leading mechanics from the Development Department – Cliff Bray, Jimmy Cox and Harold Wiggins. There was also a shy and quiet spoken tea boy by the name of Gerald Wiffen, later to become one of the team's longest serving and most experienced mechanics. One of the earliest recruits was Tommy Wellman who came from the Service Division at MG. Tommy was soon to become charge hand and to follow Doug up through the ranks as his faithful deputy. Everything was always impossible to Tom Wellman, until the chips were down and then he did as good a job as the next man. He was a great improvisor, a talented schemer for new ideas with a wealth of competitions experience to call upon. He was a likeable character and had a wide circle of chums in important positions in neighbouring factories who he could always call upon for help.

Doug Hamblin was another early recruit, this time from the

Rectification Department. He was a bold, brash character but a hard and efficient worker who very soon earned his title as deputy foreman. It was a sad day for the team when Doug lost his life in a road accident on the Monte.

Ready and very able to fill the vacant post of deputy foreman was Den Green, a brilliant mechanic who came to Abingdon from an Oxford garage. Den, particularly in later years, gained the growing respect of the team drivers as one of the most resourceful operators in the field. He inherited from Doug Watts the spirit of adventure and determination and, unlike some of his staff colleagues, he was able to keep abreast of the office paperwork (which he hated) while losing none of his skill as a practical mechanic.

It was not long before the growing Competitions team was encroaching too much upon the space of the Development Department and so Marcus Chambers and his men were moved to their own premises. They took with them another very important member of the team – storeman Neville Challis. A good storekeeper is a secret weapon in any Competitions Department and Neville was one of the best. He had a remarkable capacity to produce just what you wanted 'off the shelf' and, if he could not, then he knew just where to go and get it. Neville knew as much about other people's stores in BMC as they did, and although it was not wise to inquire too deeply into the origins of certain parts and how delivery was effected so quickly, he always ensured that the Department remained on the best of terms with its suppliers.

A new tea boy was found with the move to new premises – Bob Whittington who was soon spotted by Doug Watts as suitable talent. He progressed to become one of the most meticulous workers in the Department. Bob's place was filled by young Johnny Lay who Doug also trained into a top-class mechanic. Johnny was one of the very few in the team who did not stay and after a couple of years he emigrated to the States and set up in business on his own.

Another old-timer was Brian Moylan who, unlike his team mates, was not a Berkshireman but came from London during the war years. Brian was always serious and a great 'thinker'; he later served as Shop Steward. Nobby Hall was one of the old Abingdon road testers in Doug Watts's time but he only joined Competitions after a spell away from Abingdon when he tried to set up in business on his own. Nobby is a craftsman rather than a mechanic, one of the finest metal workers and welders in the business, and he found his niche in later years working on the development and testing of new models for competitions.

After a brief trip to America, the team was happy to welcome back Cliff Humphries who would be right at the top of the list of anyone who had the difficult job of selecting the best all-rounder in the team. In later years his acknowledged skill as an engine builder led him to become our Chief Technician, entirely responsible for the development and testing programme of new ideas and new models.

The work of the Department attracted people with the widest possible interest and Johnny Organ was certainly one of them. His father owned a sweet shop in Oxford and young Johnny was a professional boxer before he came to Abingdon. He later became an authority on rare horticulture and is now an author of technical motoring books. Roy Brown had unusual hobbies too for he was a lay preacher.

To assist Marcus Chambers in the office a young Commercial Apprentice by the name of Bill Price came to Abingdon. Bill was a tower of strength to Marcus, Stuart Turner and myself, his particular speciality being the complicated homologation of new models and new parts. In his later years he took on more responsibilities and led the team on many successful sorties commanding respect from everyone in the team.

For the rest of the team, Doug Watts selected a succession of apprentices who came into the Department as part of their training and showed particular ability as mechanics. Amongst those who stayed on to become fully skilled fitters were Peter Bartram, Dudley Pike, Tommy Eales, Robin Vokins, Mick Legg, Mick Hogan and Gordon Bisp. From the former Service Department came Johnny Evans, Frank Rudman and their chief tester Eddie Burnell. Years of handling competition cars made Eddie a superb driver and on more than one occasion he proved that he was faster around our favourite Bagshot test track than even Paddy Hopkirk! The team was completed by panel beater, Stan Bradford, an electrician Derek Argyle. John Smith of Lucas must also be considered as a fully fledged member of the team for he served regular spells at Abingdon.

Last but not least were the long-suffering secretaries who somehow managed to keep pace with the ever changing travel schedules on events and the always elusive Competition Managers. Margaret Hall and Jane Derrington served Marcus Chambers, Diana Kirkby survived the whole of Stuart Turner's reign while Mary Smith and Sandy Lawson made my spell in the 'hot seat' a great deal easier.

This then was the team that was to make the name of Abingdon as well known in rallying circles as M G s pre-war competition achievements had done through racing and record breaking. From its earliest days there was generated a unique spirit between management, staff, mechanics and drivers. This undoubtedly came about by the way Marcus Chambers and Doug Watts established a working atmosphere where everyone in the team played an equally responsible role and was thus treated with equal respect. While the team managers and the drivers of rival teams stayed in only the best hotels and the mechanics had to make do with second-rate accommodation, the B M C team made a point of travelling together, staying in the same hotels, eating at the same table and drinking at the same bar. Only in this way did everyone from the number one driver and the team manager to the rawest apprentice gain each other's respect, friendship and confidence. When three people have to travel 3,000 non-stop miles together in the confines of a motor car through foreign lands they very soon learn how to get on with each other!

That they all did get on so well was probably due to the fact that practically everyone in the team was born and bred a Berkshireman. Whether all the local men are such closely-knit, determined and easy-going folk I don't know, but certainly all of those in the B M C team had these qualities. That they also turned out to be first-class mechanics seemed to be taken for granted for none came into the Department with any specialized knowledge or experience in the preparation of competition cars.

While much of the credit for the moulding of the team spirit must go to Marcus Chambers and Doug Watts, there is no doubt that the first team leader, John Gott, was also responsible for bringing a very professional and organized approach to the team's operation in the field. John had a wealth of rallying experience, true enthusiasm for the sport and his police background gave him the manner and authority to gain the ear of his team mates.

Although B M C in its heyday probably spent more on competitions than its rivals, the Abingdon team never had unlimited finances with which to operate. The nature of its activities within a production factory also meant that it could not always conform to the everyday working factory routine and abide by the trade union rule book. It was very useful, therefore, to have a strong ally within the factory

CHAPTER 2

850 DAYS

There was no wild enthusiasm for the Mini when the first 850 appeared in the Abingdon Competitions shop in the late summer of 1959. Doug Watts recalls even refusing to borrow it to go down to the local bank because he did not wish to be seen in 'such an insignificant little car'. Just as the general public's initial reaction was that this could not be considered as a 'real' car, so Abingdon almost rejected it in its early days as a suitable weapon for competition.

Many are the claims as to who was the first to realize the potential of the Mini in competitions but amongst the first to win a club rally in one was the then insignificant team of Pat Moss and Stuart Turner who entered the Knowldale Car Club's Mini Miglia. Despite the fact that they won by some 10 minutes, Pat complained that she found the Mini desperately slow while Stuart reported that it was darned uncomfortable!

However, they did a lot better than the three-car team that was entered for the 1959 RAC Rally in November with drivers 'Tish' Ozanne, Alick Pitts and Ken James. None of the cars finished for all suffered with the early problem of slipping clutches. The team did not fare very much better on the Portuguese Rally in December when two cars were entered for Nancy Mitchell and Peter Riley. This was the notoriously unsporting event when the results were decided by three driving tests and then all the 'winners' were disqualified for having the wrong coloured competition numbers and the local drivers received the victor's trophies. Despite more clutch troubles, however, both the Minis did last the distance on this occasion.

As usual when a new model arrives to be evaluated for competitions, the dirty work of finding out the troubles falls to the up and coming drivers rather than the regular works crews. This was the case with the Mini, and while only the 'men' were allowed to handle the 'big Healeys' the 'boys' played with the new Minis.

Amongst those who regularly drove the early 850s was 'Tish' Ozanne who, for some reason, hates to be called by her real name of

Pat. She had formerly been a successful private entrant in an A40 and teamed up with Pat Allison, sister of racing driver Cliff Allison, to form a very efficient and popular partnership. Nancy Mitchell was another of the early Mini drivers although better remembered for her performances with the earlier Magnettes and MGAs. Peter Riley's driving style was rather better suited to the Mini than his enormous size (he was nicknamed 'The Bear'). Peter served a good apprenticeship on the 850s before moving on to greater things with the 'big Healey'. He was later, of course, to marry Ann Wisdom.

There was not much consideration given to the co-driver's responsibilities at this time, until a young Oxford student by the name of Tony Ambrose joined the team. Tony was the first of the truly professional co-drivers who brought a lot of advanced thinking to Abingdon in the early days of the Department and was instrumental in pioneering more serious pre-event recces, pace notes and practicing. Tony's long stay with the team was rewarded with the European Rally Championship win with Rauno Aaltonen in 1965 and his record equals that of Henry Liddon as the most successful co-driver in the team. In more recent years he has found relief from the home decorating shops that he runs in Hampshire and Wiltshire to serve as organizer of the London to Sydney Marathon and the World Cup Rally.

1960–first season

The Mini was being taken a little more seriously by the time the 1960 Monte Carlo Rally came around for six cars were entered for the winter classic. Peter Riley, Don Morley and Alick Pitts were entered in the improved series class while Tom Wisdom, Nancy Mitchell and 'Tish' Ozanne drove in the standard car class. The results indicated improved reliability for only the ladies teams failed to finish.

For Alick Pitts and Tony Ambrose, however, it was an eventful journey to Monte. Starting from Paris, the dreaded clutch slip started on the first night and did not respond to the frequent injection of fire extinguisher fluid. Sand was then added to the mixture in an attempt to lock the whole thing solid. They struggled on to the Massif Central where, in thick fog, Alick ran into the back of another competitor. The accident pushed the radiator out of line and the car spun across the road knocking the rear wheel badly out of line. The damage was hastily repaired and the determined crew pressed on until the

CHAPTER 3

TURNER'S TEAM

Towards the end of the 1961 season two very significant happenings were to affect the fortunes of the B M C team. The Mini-Cooper was announced in September and, one month later, Stuart Turner became Competitions Manager.

The arrival of the Mini-Cooper came about as a result of the combined enthusiasms of John Cooper and Alec Issigonis. They managed to persuade the B M C Board that considerable prestige could come from the association with the then very successful Cooper Car Company. Drawing upon the basic experiences of the Formula Junior version of the 'A' series engine, the Mini-Cooper did not involve a great deal of new design work, but the instant decision to build the new car upon only the sporting hunch of two 'enthusiasts' is not likely to happen again in the big-time league of the British motor industry.

Stuart Turner would be the first to admit that he could not have arrived on the Abingdon scene at a better moment. Marcus Chambers had built up a superb team of mechanics that were already acknowledged as the best in the business. There were some good drivers and co-drivers under contract and the opportunity was ripe to try the talents of the rising stars from Scandinavia. The 'big Healey' was established in winning form and now the Mini-Cooper could hardly fail to bring further success.

Stuart studied accountancy until he caught the rally bug. He did his national service with the R A F where he learnt little of use other than Russian. In club rallying he was a demon navigator, winning the 'Autosport' Navigators' Trophy in 1957, 1958 and 1959. He had driven with the works teams of Auto Union, Mercedes, Saab, Triumph and B M C, his most notable success being with Erik Carlsson when they won the R A C Rally in 1960. Before he came to Abingdon he did a spell as rallies editor of *Motoring News* and wrote a best-selling book *Rallying* (Foulis, 1960).

Stuart is a born leader of men, and he would get to the top in any direction in which his ambition lay; his moves are swift and deliberate. He has an incredibly alert brain that can cut through the irrelevances of the moment and look further than most into the future. As far as motor sport is concerned his forecasts are not often wrong. He has a blunt outspokenness which some find disconcerting but he has no time for 'bumblers', petty officialdom and time wasting, indecisive committees. He is always studious, seldom smiles, has a dry sarcastic wit and keeps his friendships with his team mates at arm's length so that they may always respect his commands. His reign at Abingdon unquestionably established him as the most successful competition manager of all time.

The first Mini win

The first outing of the new Mini-Cooper was on the 1962 Monte Carlo Rally. Pat Moss and Ann Wisdom drove 737 ABL, the Mini that was to serve them so well and that first demonstrated the potential of the Cooper. But, on this event, the car was hastily prepared and only arrived at Abingdon a couple of weeks before the start. Despite a broken throttle cable in the middle of a stage, Pat and Ann won the Coupe des Dames, the first time that the Trophy, first awarded in 1927, had been won three times running by the same crew.

A significant if not successful Monte entry that year was the works-supported Mini of Geoff Mabbs with his then little-known partner, Rauno Aaltonen. Lying second overall to Erik Carlsson, Rauno crashed on the Turini and the car, upside down, caught fire. Geoff, himself badly burnt, rescued an unconscious Rauno from the blaze. In this dramatic fashion began Rauno's long and distinguished period with the team.

After this demonstration of what could be done with the Mini, it was not expected to be very long before victory fell to 'the little box'. And appropriately it was the ladies who brought that first Mini win – Pat Moss and Ann Wisdom dominating the 1962 Tulip Rally in 737 ABL. The girls set the fastest time in their class to win by a comfortable margin on the class improvement system. Minis, in fact, took the first eight places in the 1000 cc class.

Ann Wisdom, having now become Mrs Peter Riley, Pauline Mayman took over the co-driver's seat with Pat Moss. The new partnership, again with the faithful 737 ABL, emerged as worthy

also a most efficient travelling marshal on the London to Mexico World Cup Rally.

Timo Makinen

When the Minis won the team prize on the 1962 RAC Rally, amongst the names of the winning crews was the then little-known Finn, Timo Makinen (or, as one national newspaper once called him, the well-known Scottish driver Tim MacKinnen!).

Whilst I suspect that Stuart Turner did not really need any more talent to support his already strong team, he was one of the first to realize that it's better to have Timo drive for you than against you!

Timo Makinen has been, is, and will be for a very long time, the fastest rally driver in the world – if not the most successful. He has that incredible ability to get into any car and drive it over any sort of rally country faster than any other rally driver. Given unknown conditions, rally roads or race track, I would put my money on Timo against any driver. Many top drivers will recall with sheer amazement a ride with 'the big Finn'.

Just about every event that Timo drove with BMC, if he did not win, he retired with mechanical trouble when in the lead. But this should not infer that he was a car wrecker. Although he was harder on his cars than were his team mates, he had that little edge over his rivals and thus always demanded that little bit more from his cars. He was employed as a trail blazer and as such he was supreme. How often, in their pursuit of the flying Makinen, did the opposition break up too, allowing one of the other Abingdon cars to move up and win?

Timo started rallying in 1960 with a Mini prepared by the Finnish BMC Distributors with whom he formed a long-lasting association. When he first came to Abingdon he spoke very little English and he communicated with the team in a mixture of English and Finnish, which was very soon named 'Finglish'. In those early days he was a pretty irresponsible character, a big, fun-loving, playboy, always the practical joker and not very keen on hard work. Today he is as conscientious as the next man which is shown by his more relaxed and calculated performances.

It is little known that in 1966/7 Timo suffered from terrible eczema all over his body when the very worst thing for him to be doing with such a complaint was to sit for a long time in hot, sweaty racing overalls. It was typical of Timo's determination that he kept this very much to himself, shrugged off the discomfort and considerable pain and continued to drive as competitively as ever.

We shall, I feel, in years to come look back on Timo Makinen with the same awe and respect that now surrounds the great Juan Manuel Fangio – a driver whose fellow competitors always acknowledge as being just that little bit faster than anyone else.

Paddy Hopkirk

It was on the 1963 Monte Carlo Rally that the name of Paddy Hopkirk was first associated with the Mini – the start of a driver/car combination that was soon to prove more famous than that of the great Erik Carlsson with Saab.

Paddy came to Abingdon principally to drive the 'big Healey' which he did very well – but he drove the Mini a whole lot better. He came to BMC after very successful seasons with Rootes and Standard Triumph, but most of his driving had been on tarmac roads. Like his transition from rear-wheel drive to front-wheel drive, he soon found that he was a lot more competitive on the loose.

Paddy is the only British motor sporting personality, other than Stirling Moss, to make his name a household word. His good humour, quick wit, flashing smile, treacly Irish voice and a name that rolls off the tongue, have all helped. But Paddy has worked hard at personal promotion, right from the days when he started competition driving in 1950 while studying engineering at Trinity College, Dublin. Today he is sensibly capitalizing on his success as Chairman of the flourishing Mill Accessory Group, by broadcasting, television work, writing books and features.

Paddy is as meticulous in the way he runs his business, his dress, his driving, his manners and his personal promotion as he is about the preparation of his cars. He is sometimes finicky and can drive a mechanic to exasperation, but this is only in the pursuit of ultimate perfection in all that he does. Nothing gets under his skin more than to find that his car may not in some respect be quite as good as his team mates'.

Perhaps the qualities that have most contributed to his success are that he is a 'trier' from the drop of the flag. And it does not matter whether it's an unimportant practice day at Silverstone, a televised rallycross with seven million viewers or the final and decisive stage of a big rally. Paddy will always give of his best behind the wheel, whatever the rewards. He's brilliant too at nursing a sick car home to

in winning both the Coupe des Dames and a Coupe des Alpes while Terry Hunter and Henry Liddon in a private Mini helped to win the Team Prize.

While the 1071 could not have done better on the Alpine, the team's performance on the Tour de France saw the first occasion that the Mini really hit the European headlines. Paddy Hopkirk with Henry Liddon not only got up amongst the big Ford Galaxies and Jaguars to come third in the touring category but they finished third overall on scratch and won the much-publicized handicap category.

It is always hard to find tangible proof that competition successes sell motor cars but Paddy's achievement on this event is down on record as having sparked off a remarkable sales impact for the Mini in France. The BMC dealer in Montpellier reported having taken orders for nine Mini-Coopers before the event was over while the main Paris distributor placed orders for three times his annual Mini quota at the London Motor Show.

But not all the interest was abroad and Paddy, now in brilliant form, came home for the RAC Rally to be placed fourth overall, the top British finisher and not very far behind the leading Scandinavians, Tom Trana, Harry Kallstrom and Erik Carlsson. Paddy, in fact, was fastest, or equal fastest, over 20 of the 39 special stages.

The Mini from Minsk

With the 1071, the mechanics, the drivers – and Paddy Hopkirk in particular – on top form, things were shaping up for the team's first big-time win. And the brilliance of the Abingdon team could not have been better rewarded than with their first Monte victory in 1964.

The team of 1071s included Paddy Hopkirk, Timo Makinen, Rauno Aaltonen and Pauline Mayman. The BBC's Raymond Baxter (later to serve for a short period as BMC's Director of Publicity) completed the team in a Group 3 997 car. Paddy's win was a closely fought battle against the opposition and the handicap system. Starting from Minsk in Russia with co-driver Henry Liddon, Paddy by no means had the easiest run or the best of the weather. The navigation in Russia was not easy and Paddy recalls one nasty moment when they went the wrong way and had to do a very quick handbrake turn when faced by an unfriendly military gentleman described as a 'tea cosy with a sten gun poking out'!

Paddy was also in trouble in France when by mistake he shot up a one-way street. An angry gendarme appeared on the scene and demanded that he presented his road book for the breach of the traffic regulations to be recorded, an entry which would have un-undoubtedly disqualified him from the Rally. But the cunning Irish-man declared that he had not got his road book because he had retired from the Rally and was hurrying home to attend the funeral of a close relative. The gendarme looked disbelieving, recorded Paddy's name and details of the car and finally sent the crew on their way. Paddy was always dying to see the expression on that gendarme's face when next morning he read that a certain Monsieur Hopkirk in car registra-tion number 33 EJB had won the Rally!

The popularity of the first Monte victory was undoubtedly height-ened by the David and Goliath battle between the diminutive Minis and the massive team of Ford Falcons who had openly declared that they were going to conquer rallying's greatest prize. Despite the performance of Ford's racing drivers, Bo Ljungfeldt, Jo Schlesser, Henri Greder and Graham Hill, and the ever-present threat of Erik Carlsson's Saab, Paddy led his Finnish team mates to a marginal but glorious victory and Abingdon again took home the Team Prize. It was a superlative performance not only to beat the handicap formula, and the big capacity opposition but also to gain victory over mainly dry roads which gave no advantage to front-wheel-drive cars. So close in fact was the contest that when Paddy was awakened from his slumbers and told that he had won, he took a great deal of persuading that he had won outright and not just won his class!

Enter the 1275 and 970

The 1071 Cooper 'S' was designed with yet further engine develop-ments in mind and in March 1964 two new versions became available. By fitting a long-stroke crankshaft a 1275 cc (75 bhp) version was provided and by the use of a short-stroke crankshaft the capacity was reduced to 970 cc (68 bhp). The smaller engine was conceived with the one litre class of the European Saloon Car Championship in mind while the 1275 version was the obvious evolution of the 'A' series unit to within the limitations of the 1300 cc class limit for both racing and rallying.

The new-found power of the 1275 was very soon put to good effect. First time out, and with the new model only just homologated, Timo Makinen claimed outright victory on the Tulip Rally, again just

Easter–mind over Makinen

Another brilliant co-driver started his long and successful association
with the team at this time – a young garage proprietor from Stony
Stratford – Paul Easter.

His first drive with the team on the 1964 Tour de France came as a
result of a last-minute panic when Paul was called in to replace Timo
Makinen's original co-driver, Don Barrow, who was taken ill. For
Paul that first outing was a co-driver's nightmare. Coming into
Grenoble on the last day of the event, when they were lying well-
placed, Paul was driving with Timo stretched out asleep in the passenger's seat. A car shot out of a side turning, Paul swerved across the
road, hit the kerb, the Mini darted back across the road and ended
up as a write-off against a kilometre post. Timo woke up with a grunt,
surveyed the wreckage, turned to the quivering Paul and said, 'I
think we go find nice pub and you buy me big drink!'

Clearly there were no repercussions to this incident for the Makinen–
Easter crew went on to become one of the closest and best-matched
partnerships in rallying. As is so often the case, the fact that they were
such opposites contributed a great deal to their ability to work together
so effectively. Timo, in those days, desperately needed a steadying
influence to his driving and although Paul seemed the one most un-
likely to succeed, in fact it proved to be the ideal match.

Paul started rallying in 1961 as a driver in an 850 and he got his trial
run with the team as a result of his class winning performance in the
1963 Acropolis Rally – no mean achievement with a private Mini.
Paul was one of the most meticulous and 'deep-thinking' co-drivers
in the team but it was also his exceptional ability as a Mini driver that
found him favour with Timo.

It is the basic aspects of competition Mini driving that we look at in
the following chapter.

CHAPTER 5

MINI DRIVING

If you have ever watched the leading rally drivers in action, either on a rally special stage or on film, you will undoubtedly have been impressed by their speed but perhaps puzzled by their technique. The Scandinavians were responsible for introducing this style of driving into Europe and Rauno Aaltonen and Timo Makinen in their works Minis were amongst the first to demonstrate their art outside of their native Finland.

The technique, some claim, was evolved in the days when nearly all Scandinavians drove Saabs, which have front-wheel-drive and which used to be fitted with a free-wheel device. The art of left-foot braking started with these cars and one of the earliest exponents was the great Erik Carlsson. The 'sideways' technique was both impressive and effective in the Saab, but a lot more so when applied to a car with the handling and performance characteristics of the Mini.

Paddy Hopkirk is undoubtedly the British driver who has best acquired the Scandinavian's art and he has provided the most coherent description of the theory of how it's done. The following explanation is partly taken from an interview with Paddy after the 1964 Monte.

Whereas front-wheel-drive is generally accepted as safer than rear-wheel-drive for the ordinary motorist, most enthusiast drivers of the older generation probably favour rear-wheel-drive to get them out of a sticky position. But, after the early successes of front-wheel-drive cars in rallies and the demonstrations of the Scandinavian driving technique, many more keen drivers now favour front-wheel-drive.

It is not generally appreciated that the more power the front-wheel-drive car has the better the technique works. But, of course, this only holds true when the car is in the hands of an expert who knows exactly how to utilize the power in the right manner. It is also important that the technique is practised in a car which is inherently well balanced on corners.

Two facts make the front-wheel-drive car a better proposition for the expert in emergencies. You can play the brakes against the accelerator for combined braking and steering, which is the basis of left-foot braking. Furthermore, you need not lose control of the car even if the tail swings out far beyond a point where most rear-wheel-drive cars would be irretrievably lost.

These principles may be more easily understood if we consider some illustrated examples and weigh them against what could be done, or rather not be done, in a rear-wheel-drive car in the same situations.

Looking at figure 1, if the angle *b* (which represents the angle of the car against the direction of travel) gets bigger during a slide than angle

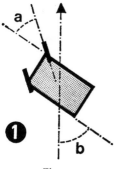

Fig. 1

a (which represents the maximum steering lock), the rear-wheel-drive car cannot be prevented from spinning helplessly around. With the powerful front-wheel-drive car you can make the front end move faster than the rear end and thus straighten up the car.

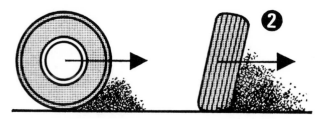

Fig. 2

On gravel (figure 2) you get more braking from wheels that move sideways than from forward-moving wheels because you get more retardation from the build-up of grit against the side of the wheel.

This was one of the reasons why racing tyres were later used on the works Minis to such good effect because the sharp shoulder of the racing tyre provided a better sideways grip under these conditions than the more rounded shoulder of the rough road tread pattern.

In figure 3 we have an emergency case in which the car has been brought up to a corner far too fast. Hard braking would simply make

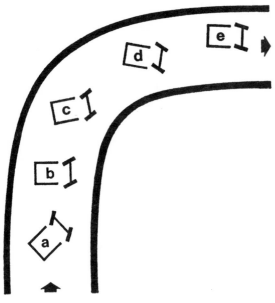

Fig. 3

the car run out of road but with front-wheel-drive it is possible to steer the car out of danger. The technique is to floor the accelerator and the brake as hard as possible without quite locking the front wheels. With full throttle you will, in this way, postpone the point of locking the driving wheels while, at the same time, locking the rear wheels. Simultaneously you flick the steering wheel slightly to the right to make the tail slide outwards as shown at point *a*. The car will now slide sideways with locked rear wheels, while the front wheels are pulling against the brakes (points *b* and *c*) as you continue to play the brakes against the accelerator. To keep the car on the road you now turn the front wheels into the corner (point *d*) still letting them pull at full power against the brakes and with the rear wheels locked.

The car is still drifting sideways at point *d* so that the front wheels will scrub against the road surface and help retard the car in the sideways direction while pulling it away from the kerb. If you have done the job properly, the car will now be well positioned for being gently straightened up on its way out of the corner at point *e*, still with the power on, but with the brakes now released.

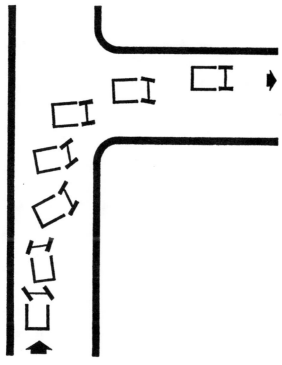

Fig. 4

A similar technique can be applied to planned fast cornering (figure 4). In this case the tail is first intentionally swung in a skid towards the inner kerb and then, through over-correcting, swung to the opposite side with the intention of retarding the car with sideways tyre-scrubbing.

On sharp corners (figure 5) it is possible to negotiate them in an even more extreme manner with front-wheel-drive cars by using power and brakes in combination.

The art of left-foot braking was expertly explained by Rauno Aaltonen in an interview with Wilson McComb, then B M C Competitions Press Officer, which appeared in one of the Castrol Achievements Books.

Rauno explained that while some people throw the car sideways before the corner to reduce the speed quickly at the last moment, he works on the principle that nine out of ten corners look a lot slower than they really are, so his technique is to go into every one just a little

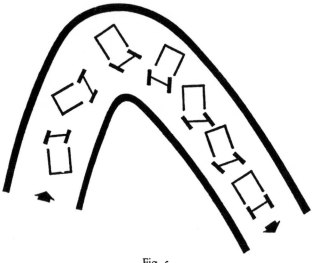

Fig. 5

bit faster than the speed which appears to be the maximum. This means that nine corners go just right but the tenth he finds that he is going just a little too fast. By the time he has realized this, it would be too late to throw the car sideways so he keeps the steering wheel in the same position, keeps the accelerator hard down but very quickly hits the brake pedal with the left foot. The pedal is not kept down but hit once, very hard. This causes the rear wheels to lock before the front because the rear wheels are running free and the front ones are still being driven. Locked wheels have very little grip so the tail begins to slide out, the car turns on its axis, and you can continue through the corner. The rear braking could, of course, be applied with the handbrake but there is seldom the time to take one's hands off the steering wheel and the handbrake is not so efficient.

The secret is that you must do this braking very quickly and have your left foot ready over the brake all the time. Then it becomes a great temptation to use it too often and Rauno recommends that if you have a close rival who is always beating you on rallies, and he does not know about left-foot braking, then you must quickly show him because until he learns to use it properly he will not trouble you again! Continuous left-foot braking on tortuous mountain roads can lead to excessive brake wear and temperature build up. Timo Makinen was particularly hard on his brakes with his style of left-foot braking and often, at service points after long special stages, the rear brakes would literally catch fire once the car stopped moving!

In considering left-foot braking for rear-wheel-drive cars, Rauno has got some interesting thoughts. Just before the corner he presses the brake to get the car to drift slightly; he is very much against cars which oversteer and likes neutral handling characteristics. By putting full power on before the corner you have the car drifting with the tail out a little. Supposing that you now find that you have estimated the speed incorrectly, the tail will slide out more, you correct by steering into the skid but soon you will come to the full lock position and the car will start to spin. This is when you can use left-foot braking. Keeping the power to the rear wheels with the right foot hard on the accelerator you hit the brake pedal hard with the left foot. The front wheels lock and slide so that the front of the car comes back to the right direction for the corner. This is, in fact, the exact reverse of the effect achieved with the front-wheel-drive car.

The other advantages of using left-foot braking with rear-wheel-drive come when you are drifting, with equal grip on all four wheels, and the inside rear wheel starts to lift. If you have no limited slip differential, this wheel will immediately start to spin, and then you will lose all the driving power to the other rear wheel. By stamping the left foot on the brake you can stop the inside rear wheel from spinning and apply more torque to the outside wheel.

Another advantage claimed by Rauno for both front- and rear-wheel-drive cars is that with the sudden application of the brakes at the right moment when cornering you can cause a twist in the suspension which locks the joints and makes them stiffer. This makes the car more stable, there is less roll, and it does not bounce about and sway so much.

Race driving

Some rally drivers have put up some spectacular performances on race tracks by applying their left-foot braking technique to circuit racing. But none have been able to match either the spectacle or the speed of the man who has been the fastest Mini racer for many years – John Rhodes.

Many so-called experts have criticized John's tyre-burning style as being excessively dramatic, but the fact remains that, given cars of equal performance, John will always be just that little bit quicker than anyone else. Because the Mini's handling has become more conventional with the later 12 in. diameter racing tyres, John's style has also changed. Because the racing Mini today handles more like a conventional racing car, John feels that his technique no longer gives him the big advantage that he could display on the 10 in. racing tyres.

The Rhodes' smoke-screen cornering technique owed nothing to left-foot braking. It was achieved by having the car set up with such balance at the entry to the corner that it was possible to put the car into the angle of drift by simply lifting the foot off the accelerator and, at the same time, giving the steering wheel a slight flick towards the apex of the corner. This had the effect of applying slight braking to the front wheels thus causing the tail to go 'light' and to break away. Braking for the corner was thus achieved by allowing the rear of the car to 'hang out' quite dramatically, and all of this could be done really deep into the corner thus gaining an advantage on your rear-wheel-drive competitors. Then the car could be controlled by steering and by throttle work, keeping the front wheels ahead of the rear. With the better grip of the later 12 in. diameter tyres, it was necessary only to let the rear of the car 'hang out' a fraction and then the car would be driven through the corner in the conventional manner. The 12 in. tyres thus demanded more conventional braking than with the 10 in. equipment.

Having tried to explain briefly the basics of these very advanced techniques, I must add that they require intense skill, years of practice and they can only be performed properly and safely in a car with adequate power, competition handling characteristics, and which is fitted with the right tyres. If you must try them for yourself, borrow someone else's Mini and go practise in the biggest field you can find!

CHAPTER 6

AALTONEN CHAMPION

For the first time for many years, the 1965 European Rally Championship presented a sensible, straightforward and worthy contest. There were 12 very good qualifying rounds and some 20 works and semi-works teams competed for the major honours. BMC, like most manufacturers, did not start the year determined to chase the Championship title but, by mid-season, it was clear that Rauno Aaltonen had a very fair chance of success and the later programme was geared to assist his win.

It was Timo Makinen, however, who hit the headlines right at the start of the season by putting up a truly sensational performance to win the Monte Carlo Rally with Paul Easter. Some measure of their performance can be judged by the fact that the Mini would have won on scratch as well as when the handicap advantage was applied.

Starting from Stockholm so as to run upon the snow-ploughed main roads and avoid the worst of the tedious and dangerous French routes, Timo and Paul ran into the notorious blizzard just before the merging points of the concentration routes at Chambery. With plenty of time in hand, most competitors bumbled along in the bad conditions, but not Timo. He drove the final kilometers flat out so that, before setting out on the run-in to Monte, he had fully tested the car's performance and handling on spiked tyres in the bad conditions.

From Chambéry onwards, the blizzard was really monstrous and crews had to fight their way through a blanket of snow so bad that all the quartz lamps in the world, heated windscreens, two-speed wipers and spiked tyres could hardly cope. Many crews got lost, fell into ditches or struck obstacles buried in the snow. Navigation was incredibly difficult because snowdrifts had covered all the landmarks and the mileage recorder was highly inaccurate because of constant wheel-spin.

That only 35 of the 237 starters reached Monte within the hour of permitted lateness to qualify as finishers was almost unprecedented and gives some idea of the severity of the event. That Timo's Mini was the only car to finish without any lateness penalties at all was amazing. That he made fastest time overall in three out of the five special stages on the final run in to Monte was astounding. For much of this time he was running as the leading car in the Rally and therefore had to path-find for the entire entry, punching through snow-drifts more than bonnet high. The snow came right over the roof and the weight of it cracked the screen on one occasion.

The 35 runners then had to take part in the 400 mile Mountain Circuit with six flat-out special stages timed to the second. At the start Timo had the equivalent of a 10 minute lead over his nearest rival Lucien Bianchi (Citroen) and Eugen Bohringer (Porsche). He could have taken things easy but Timo preferred to set his usual pace so that he could keep fully alert for the demanding conditions that lay ahead. He did, in fact, strengthen his position with a remarkable performance that set the fastest time on five out of six stages.

On the one stage he was not fastest he lost time, and very nearly the Rally, when the contact breaker spring in the distributor snapped. That Timo and Paul diagnosed the fault and changed the spring in the remarkable time of only four minutes is almost unbelievable – that would be a great effort for a skilled mechanic with all the tools ready in a well-lit garage. To do it by the side of the road in the middle of the night in a snowstorm is the work of the true professional rally driver.

The Mini's second Monte win was given worldwide acclaim by the press but no doubt it was the margin of Timo's crushing victory that set *Monegasque* minds thinking of ways and means of preventing further Mini domination. One would also imagine that they were not amused when Timo was late arriving for the formal prize presentations by Princess Grace! When Timo and Paul piled into the Mini to go and collect their trophies the car refused to start. After a quick look under the bonnet, mechanic Nobby Hall was called in and, finding no spark, he changed the coil and the plugs to no avail. On closer examination of the distributor it was discovered that when Timo had replaced the contact breaker spring, he had dropped the little fibre insulating washer that holds the spring off the base plate. Somehow the spring had stayed in place for the rest of the Mountain Circuit but, when the engine cooled down, it had slipped and shorted to earth. The Monte is not often won by such good luck!

No finishers in Sweden

After such a brilliant Monte it seemed sensible to send the Abingdon trio to another winter classic, the Swedish Rally. Hopkirk, Makinen and Aaltonen were joined by Harry Kallstrom, then driving for B M C Sweden, but it was the first of the annual abortive attempts to win with the Mini in Sweden. All four cars retired on this occasion with broken differential pinions, lack of lubrication being caused by the intense cold.

Better fortune came on the Circuit of Ireland, which Paddy won for the third year running after a tremendous battle with the Cortinas of Vic Elford and David Seigle-Morris.

The unusually severe winter conditions in Europe stayed for the Tulip Rally, much of the southern route becoming impassable and many stages having to be cancelled. The B M C team, however, were the only ones who went prepared for such conditions and the wily Stuart Turner had studded tyres all laid on for the lone works Mini of Timo Makinen.

In company with the 'big Healey' of Don Morley and the private Mini of Julian Vernaeve, these three cars completely dominated the event, the Morleys finishing on scratch just ahead of Timo with Julian in a creditable third place.

Then came a completely illogical re-classification of the entry according to the 'class improvement' system which not only took into account a competitor's performance in relation to the others in his class, but also a comparison was made between the performances of other class winners in the categories. Thus Don Morley was placed no higher than eighth overall, Timo's brilliant performance earned him nothing better than sixth overall and Julian Vernaeve came off best by winning his class in the G T category. A fine performance by the Minis, but a completely illogical result.

It's all Greek to Timo

Sometimes you can retire from a rally quickly and quite painlessly when the car suddenly stops with some mechanical fault that cannot be cured. More often, however, small troubles lead to other misfortunes and you finally stagger around the route with the car slowly falling to pieces as drama follows drama. The 1965 Acropolis Rally turned out to be just such an event for Timo Makinen and Paul Easter.

The exhaust falling off caused the first problem. There was not time to put it back on so they had to carry it in the car, Paul clutching the hot and battered pipe. It was on the next section that they smelt burning and discovered that the exhaust system had set fire to the carpets. Paul now had to fight the fire on the move and must have caused some alarm to the locals by throwing pieces of burning carpet out of the windows!

Arriving at a ferry crossing it was found that the rubber couplings needed replacing. Once the car was on the boat Timo and Paul tipped the Mini on to its side and started to dismantle the drive shafts. Meanwhile the ferry captain was going mad as petrol gushed out of the filler cap, ran down the decks and into the bilges. Arriving at the other side of the crossing the Mini was righted and wheeled on to the roadway where a donkey provided the means of pulling the Mini back on to its side to finish the job. By this time the locals were convinced that their fellow boat passengers were quite mad!

With the Mini mobile again, Timo set off and was back in the lead when the rear sub frame began to break up. A holed sump was now added to the list of damage, then the rear sub frame got so bad that the tyres began to puncture as they rubbed against the bodywork. Welding was called for at the next service point, and the Mini was again tipped on to its side. Despite careful attention to the overflowing fuel, a spark from the welding torch started a small fire and within seconds the Mini was ablaze. While Timo fought to retrieve his passport and money from the glove pocket, bystanders got the fire under control. The repairs were completed and the charred Mini again took to the road.

With only 15 cars still running there was hope that Timo could hold his slender lead. Sadly, however, the fire had melted one of the carburetters and the engine was soon only spluttering along. It finally stopped and refused to start again as the bearings had seized, probably as a result of the frequent displacement of oil during the 'tip-up' pit stops.

With but 60 miles to go, an exhausted Timo and Paul sat by the roadside and watched the survivors go by in the dust. To add to the tale of woe, Stuart Turner in his attempt to keep pace with the ailing Mini, had a monumental head-on accident with a lorry and completely wrecked his service car!

On the Championship trail

Better fortune came to Rauno Aaltonen and Tony Ambrose when they scored a runaway win on the Geneva Rally. They then claimed an equally convincing victory on the Czech Rally, this time against more serious opposition. Amassing a healthy score of Championship points, their brilliant form continued to bring victory on the Polish Rally – three outright wins within a couple of months.

The team's winning ways continued with the 1000 Lakes Rally, when Timo Makinen won for the second year in succession with Rauno Aaltonen as runner-up. Paddy Hopkirk finished a remarkable sixth overall, ahead of all the visiting Swedes, proving that he was one of the few 'foreigners' ever successfully to challenge the locals on their home ground. In Paddy's own opinion, that 1000 Lakes result was one of the most satisfying of his rallying career.

Paddy had a less rewarding outing on the German Rally – the Nordrhein-Westfalen. Although the Mini, along with team mate Andrew Hedges's M G B, between them won every special stage, the handicap system gave victory to a locally entered Opel Rekord! The road sections were highly confusing and were so arranged that only with local knowledge could one find the well-hidden controls which were placed up farm-tracks and dubious country lanes. The only timed tests included driving tests, slalom sprints, hill climbs and even a timed 'Le Mans' start.

Paddy was so outspoken against the organizers that he swore he would never compete in the event again. The organizers retaliated by saying that they would not accept his entry, so that was the last time B M C ever entered the German Rally.

Clean sweep Alpine

Only 1·7 seconds separated Timo Makinen from outright victory on the 1965 Alpine Rally but, despite this disappointment, the B M C team collected just about every other Alpine award that it was possible to win. They brought home no fewer than 27 major trophies, probably the largest and most impressive array of silverware ever won by a works team. Only eight Coupes des Alpes were awarded that year and only four went to British cars, three going to the Minis of Timo, Paddy and the new-comer to the team, Tony Fall.

Paddy realized a personal ambition by winning his Coupe, for he gained an even more coveted Alpine trophy, the Coupe d'Argent for completing three non-consecutive unpenalized Alpine runs. Another member of the team scoring a personal hat-trick was Pauline Mayman, who with Val Domleo, won the Coupe des Dames in the touring category for the third year running. The girls had a worrying time when the fanbelt began to slip eventually causing a temporary engine seizure. They came to a halt close by a small mountain stream, built a dam, filled the radiator from the windscreen washer bottle and pressed on to the control to arrive mere seconds late thus losing their Coupe des Alpes. These were the only road penalties that they lost on the whole event.

Rauno Aaltonen and Tony Ambrose had the harrowing experience of being directed by a gendarme up the wrong road just after a time control. By sheer coincidence the roadbook instructions fitted the wrong route and it was not until after 10 kms that Tony spotted the error. They retraced their steps just as fast as a 1275 Mini with 7000 rev/min on the clock would go but reached the control just 67 seconds late. They lost their Coupe but, more serious, Rauno lost his Coupe d'Or, the most precious of all Alpine awards presented for three consecutive penalty-free runs. Finally, top honours in the contest for the Team Prize went to the Minis, all six of the Abingdon-prepared cars finishing amongst the 32 survivors.

New boy–Tony Fall

The most talked about performance on the Alpine was that of Tony Fall, the keen club rally man from Yorkshire who, on his first continental event, and the first time he had driven on the right hand side of the road, won a Coupe des Alpes. When offered a works drive as a result of this performance, he immediately justified his place in the team with some instant wins that even made the regular works drivers stop calling him the up-and-coming-man. And yet after these early victories, he seemed to lapse into a less successful period when accidents through over-exuberant driving, repeated mechanical failures and just bad luck robbed him of results. This was despite the steadying influence of Mike Wood, his faithful co-driver throughout his career with B M C.

When the B M C rally team was disbanded, one hoped that Tony would find the number one works drive that he deserved after three years as number four behind the Makinen, Aaltonen, Hopkirk trio.

But, for one reason or another, Tony to date has sadly not achieved that ambition although he has amassed a vast amount of international experience driving free-lance for Lancia, Ford, Porsche and Datsun. However, if sheer enthusiasm and determination count, I have no doubt that Tony Fall, who still has many more mature years of driving to come, will in time match the achievements of the only British rally drivers to reach the top class – Paddy Hopkirk and Roger Clark.

Penultimate round

With a healthy score of points for the 1965 Championship, Rauno Aaltonen and Tony Ambrose set off for the penultimate round – the Munich–Vienna–Budapest Rally. Rauno scored a lucky win for it was his principal championship rival, Rene Trautmann, who led the Rally all the way until 50 km from the finish when he had the wretched luck to have piston failure on his Lancia.

Originally the regulations for the rally indicated that the results would be on the controversial 'class improvement' system. Furthermore, it was ruled that no servicing would be allowed. Crafty Stuart Turner rounded up some privateers to run to team orders behind Aaltonen and one crew was also instructed to sit on Rauno's tail for the whole event and give him service if necessary. This service was admirably performed by the co-drivers team of Paul Easter and Henry Liddon who went with rough road tyres so that they could swop them with Rauno's racing tyres for the forestry stages. They carried 21 gallons of fuel, the luggage for both crews and an enormous kit of tools and spares.

As things turned out the organizers had the last laugh when at the last moment they changed the regulations back to a scratch classification. However, the Easter and Liddon support crew enjoyed a magnificent rally and, despite stopping at every stage to swop tyres with Rauno and keep him in good repair, they finished second to the works car in the class.

Rauno's win now put him at the top of the Championship table and only a really outstanding drive by Rene Trautmann on the R A C Rally could rob B M C of the Championship.

Champion's R A C

Not only was there great interest in the battle for the Championship result on the R A C Rally but there was considerable speculation within the BMC camp as to whether Timo Makinen, who chose a 'big Healey', would beat his Mini-mounted team mate, Rauno Aaltonen. The fact that both were in different classes did not jeopardize Rauno's chances for the Championship, and the struggle between the two Finns proved to be the sensation of the Rally.

Rauno had the strongest possible support team, works Minis being in the hands of Paddy Hopkirk, Tony Fall, Harry Kallstrom and the dapper little Finn, Jorma Lusenius. Jorma had earned his works drive as a result of his outstanding performance on the 1000 Lakes Rally in a Mini entered by BMC Sweden.

Timo, in typical style, set off to establish an incredible lead until an off-the-road episode on one of the snowy Yorkshire stages put him right out of the running. But almost unbelievably he fought back to such good effect that he was back in the lead by the time the Rally reached Wales. Meanwhile, Rauno had been playing a waiting game and such was the pace of the Healey and the leading Minis of Aaltonen, Lusenius and Hopkirk that most of the works opposition had dropped out, including the only other Championship contender, Rene Trautmann.

Now all interest was centred on the contest between the two Finns as the cars tackled the steep snowy slopes of the Welsh stages. It was under such atrocious conditions that the lighter front-wheel-drive car had the advantage and, although it was undoubtedly one of Timo's finest drives, Rauno just managed to scramble through to win.

So for the first time a British car won the European Championship, a fitting reward for the partnership of Rauno Aaltonen and Tony Ambrose who claimed five out of the team's eight wins of the season. Without doubt it had been the busiest and the most successful year for any works team.

The 850 Mini made an undramatic entry into international rallying and, while the regular works teams were winning with the 'big Healeys', selected private owners were loaned works cars. *Above*, 'Tish' Ozanne and Nicky Gilmour on the 1959 R A C Rally. *Below*, Tommy Gold and Mike Hughes, class winners on the 1960 Alpine Rally

Scurrying along on the 1960 Alpine Rally, and with little time to admire the
scenery, Alick Pitts and Tony Ambrose

In the days when the R A C Rally included comic tests like wiggle woggles on skid pans David Seigle-Morris with his intrepid co-driver, Vic Elford, slithers his way to sixth place overall on the 1960 event

The 1961 Monte Carlo Rally team, all smiles outside the M G Factory before the start. They did not smile for long for all three cars failed to finish. *Left to right*, Peter Garnier/Rupert Jones (accident with a non–competing car), Tom Christie/ Ninian Patterson (food poisoning), Derek Astle/Steve Woolley (hit a landslide)

Peter Riley and Tony Ambrose on their way to a class win on the 1961 Tulip Rally, the last significant outing for the 850 Mini before the arrival of the Mini-Cooper

Interior of the early works 850 Minis was functional if not as professional as on the later Mini-Coopers. The mechanic here is Johnny Organ, now a successful author of car maintenance and servicing manuals

The first of the works Mini-Coopers, 737 ABL, immediately showed the potential of the new model. Pat Moss and Ann Wisdom won the Coupe des Dames on the 1962 Monte Carlo Rally *(above)* and went on to win, in the same car, the Tulip Rally *(below)* and the German Rally

Two newcomers to the team having their first Mini drives, Timo Makinen *(above)* on the 1962 R A C Rally in which he won the touring class, and Paddy Hopkirk *(below)* setting off on the 1963 Monte Carlo Rally

Early days for two of rallying's most successful partnerships. *Above*, Rauno Aaltonen with Tony Ambrose (third overall on the 1963 Monte Carlo Rally). *Below*, Paddy Hopkirk and Henry Liddon (second overall on the 1963 Tulip Rally). Both are seen driving 997 Mini-Coopers

Carrying on where Pat Moss left off, Pauline Mayman with Val Domleo (997 Mini-Cooper) leave on the 1963 Alpine Rally to win the first of three consecutive Alpine Coupes des Dames

First international outing for the 1071 Mini-Cooper 'S' was on the 1963 Alpine Rally. Rauno Aaltonen and Tony Ambrose climb the Col de la Cayolle to score a dominating win in the touring category

A little bit of trackmanship by Timo Makinen (No. 27) helps Paddy Hopkirk score his sensational handicap win with the 1071 Mini-Cooper 'S' on the 1963 Tour de France

An equally impressive result for Paddy Hopkirk and the 1071 Mini Cooper 'S' was fourth overall on the 1963 R A C Rally

Engine room of the 1071 Mini-Cooper 'S' which in 1964 claimed the first Mini victory in the Monte Carlo Rally in the hands of Paddy Hopkirk

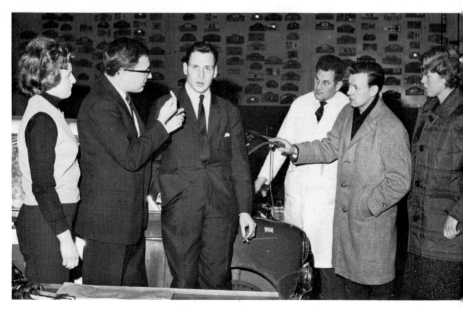

Competitions shop conference before the start of the 1964 Monte Carlo Rally. *Left to right*, Pauline Mayman, Stuart Turner, Timo Makinen, Doug Watts (Shop Supervisor), Rauno Aaltonen and Val Domleo

With the arrival of the 1275 Mini-Cooper 'S' the stage was set for the BMC team to start an unprecedented run of victories in international rallies. The partnership of Rauno Aaltonen and Tony Ambrose, seen here on their way to a touring category win on the 1964 Alpine Rally, claimed more wins than any other crew

Cockpit of the 1964 Monte Carlo Rally winner. Behind the magnifying glass is the Halda tripmaster instrument. Note the perspex shield fitted inside the the Triplex heated windscreen to improve demisting. The brake servo is mounted above the co-driver's knees!

Not only a publicity stunt for Lansing Bagnall fork lift trucks but a practical aid to servicing on the 1964 R A C Rally

An early picture of the Competitions Department staff and mechanics. *Left to right*, Brian Moylan, Nobby Hall (kneeling), Bob Whittington, Tommy Eales, Neville Challis, Cliff Humphries, Tommy Wellman (seated), Johnny Lay, Peter Bartram, Harry Carnegie, Johnny Organ, Doug Watts (seated), Roy Brown, Den Green, Doug Hamblin (seated), Bill Price, Ernie Giles, Gerald Wiffen (kneeling)

The only Mini ever to finish the gruelling Spa-Sofia-Liège Rally, John Wadsworth and Mike Wood on the 1964 Marathon

Paddy Hopkirk uses all of the road to win the Circuit of Ireland with Terry Harryman in 1965. He won, again with Terry, in 1967 and was runner-up with Tony Nash in 1969

Immaculate line astern for scrutineering on the 1965 Alpine Rally – Paddy Hopkirk, Pauline Mayman and Timo Makinen

Vigorous destruction testing in Wales during the 1965 season. *Left*, Tony Fall finds a suitable sump-crushing track

Hurrying on to victory on the 1965 R A C Rally, Rauno Aaltonen and Tony Ambrose. *Below*, they celebrate their Rally Championship win

CHAPTER 7

MINI MECHANICS

Those who are interested in the technical aspects of the works Minis will probably appreciate having all this information together in one chapter rather than dotted about in the story of the competition achievements. The most significant aspects of the preparation of the works 850, 997, 1071 and 1275 models are therefore reviewed in this chapter. It is only possible to cover the subject very broadly and any owner interested in preparing his car for competition work is advised to contact the British Leyland Special Tuning Department at Abingdon which can supply up-to-date tuning sheets for all models. It also sells all homologated Mini parts and the workshops there are able to undertake the tuning of customers' cars.

It should be emphasized that the build sheets reproduced in the following pages were selected as typical examples of the works cars as they were prepared at Abingdon for the events of the period to be eligible for the Appendix J regulations applicable for each event. Since those days there have been many changes in the regulations and a lot of new thinking on many aspects of tuning. This is, therefore, a historical report on Mini tuning as applied to the works cars, not an up-to-date guide for present-day owners. Particular reference is made to modifications that were first carried out by the Competitions Department which led to later modifications on the production model.

The 850 Mini

The early 850s were very little modified from the standard specification and, like the other rally cars of the day, preparation consisted mainly of the careful selection and assembly of standard components. There were very few special parts available and the cars had, in any case, to be very close to standard production specification when running in the touring car category.

There was little development in the early days apart from experiments to put right known weaknesses or faults that continually occurred on events. As the 850 could only hope to compete for class awards, and it was often quick enough to beat most of the class opposition of the day, there was no need for an increase in performance. Mechanical reliability was all that was necessary, coupled with suspension durability for rough road events.

The early power units were hand-built at Abingdon with transmissions being provided ready-built from Longbridge. There was no test bed available in those days and no rolling road to check performances. Indeed, testing the cars was pretty elementary by modern standards.

'We took the cars up the road to the local golf course,' recalls Cliff Humphries. 'We gave them full stick along the flat, starting opposite an A A box. If they pulled 5,800 rpm in top by the end of the straight, that was good enough. If they pulled any more it was probably a faulty rev counter!'

The first 850s used Weslake modified cylinder heads, mainly because Longbridge had a long-standing engine development contract with that company and any work done for Abingdon could be conveniently 'lost' on that budget. Towards the end of the first year of competition with the Mini, an evaluation exercise was carried out on various cylinder heads which subsequently led to the use of Don Moore modified heads for all future 850s.

Speedwell valves of improved material but standard dimensions were used and the compression ratio was increased to 9:1. Carburetter tuning was quite basic, but on the later Don Moore heads a special inlet manifold was used, the carburetter flange being cut off at the manifold and turned upside down to improve the flow.

The standard camshaft was retained on early cars but later Derek Frost at Engines Branch produced the 630 profile, the same cam form as the 148 camshaft later used on the Mini-Cooper 'S'. The standard crankshaft and flywheel assembly was used but carefully balanced. Because the standard single crankcase breather used to discharge a lot of oil, this was replaced by twin breathers.

Clutch oil seals caused many problems on the early 850 and 997 cars and modified oil seals with steel casings and retaining plates did a lot to solve these troubles. Solid steel timing chain sprockets were later introduced along with idler gears made from a solid forging. Early gearbox casings were in magnesium and, when these were replaced by aluminium ones on the production car, Abingdon acquired most of the magnesium stock and these were always used on the rally cars.

The suspension on the 850 suffered mainly from shock-absorber failures and breakages of the shock-absorber mounting brackets. Competition specifications did much to improve the life of the units and the modified front brackets, designed and developed by Abingdon, were later incorporated in the production car. The same applied to the replacement of the old bushes in the rear suspension swing arm with needle roller bearings.

The following build sheet is for one of the early works 850s built for the 1959 R A C Rally and driven by 'Tish' Ozanne. Power output would have been around 42 bhp.

Check compression ratio 9 to 1
Fit Weslake gas-flowed cylinder head
Petrol test valves
Check oil way not breaking through cylinder head
Fit Speedwell valves
Fit Speedwell valve springs
Fit air cleaner less element
Fit E3 needles
Fit Sprite dashpot and needles
Fit 0·070 in. dampers
Cut off and solder carburetter butterfly screws
Set tappets 0·015 in. hot
Strip and overhaul carburetter
Fit 74 degs thermostat
Fit radiator blind
Fit balanced crankshaft and flywheel assembly
Fit standard camshaft
Fit Vandervell bearing, white metal (mains) lead indium (big ends)
Line up connecting rods
Fit Reynolds timing chain
Fit new oil filter element
Match manifolds to ports
Check pistons and rings
Fit N3 fixed top plugs
Fit HA12 coil
Fit dual crankcase breathers
Fit 10 lb radiator cap and wire on
Check dynamo fixing and fit flat washers to bolts
Check starter motor
Overhaul distributor (type D3A/H4-LT-18047)
Check battery and charge
Fix washer to dipstick and paint white
Fit guide tube to dipstick hole
Check for oil leaks
Fit magnesium sump casings

Fit modified bottom end
Fit selected differential assembly
Fit oil seal retaining plate to flywheel
Fit standard fan
Fit hard engine mounting rubbers
Fit modified engine-steady ferrule
Check engine number plate
Fit standard primary gear
Check oil pressure to 55 lb maximum
Check clutch adjustment to 0·060 in.
Modify accelerator pedal for heel-and-toe operation
Blank off the off-side half of the front grille
Cut front grille down the centre
Fit special clutch oil seal
Check drive shafts and grease
Fit strengthener plate to the differential housing for exhaust bracket
Seal all holes in the clutch housing
Remove nylon pad and spring from gear lever linkage
Overhaul complete front suspension
Overhaul complete rear suspension
Fit new shock absorbers all round
Fit latest type top rubbers to rear shock absorbers
Fit competition exhaust system
Check all exhaust hangers
Modify rear exhaust hanger
Modify front exhaust hanger
Grease all round
Remove over riders
Increase ride height front and rear with 0·100 in. washer
Modify front shock absorber bracket
Fit latest type front suspension tie rods
Check and overhaul complete steering
Modify steering wheel nut
Track front wheels (toe out $\frac{1}{16}$ in)
Track rear wheels (toe out $\frac{1}{8}$ in)
Check camber and castor angles
Overhaul front and rear brakes, thoroughly clean wheel cylinders
Fill brake system with heavy duty fluid
Fit AM4 linings and bed in
Fit 250 lb limiting valve
Cover brake pipes where necessary
Modify handbrake to fly-off operation
Waterproof front and rear brake back plates
Remove petrol tank and flush out
Blank off breather pipe and vent cap
Protect fuel gauge tank attachment wires
Fit latest type petrol pump and clean filter
Fit Zenith filter

Fit quick-release petrol cap
Check laminated windscreen fitted
Fit GB sign to rear
Fit stick-on registration letters
Fit Tudor windscreen washer
Fit Elopress
Fit small fire extinguisher
Fit Scotchlite tape to rear bumpers and door shuts
Fit map stowages division to near-side door pockets
Fit grab handle above near-side door
Fit Union Jacks on each side of the car
Check doors for draughts and waterproof
Water test car and seal as necessary
Make provision for fitting rally plates
Fit perspex side and rear windows
Fit bonnet safety strap
Modify bonnet release
Fit protection for door lock catch
Blank off side vent in heater
Fit clips to heater duct pipes
Modify heater air duct vents
Fit padding to door pockets and pillars
Fit passenger's Barnacle mirror
Blank off all holes in bulkhead
Fit wind operated horns
Fit passenger horn button
Fit rubber mats to front of car with fasteners
Modify sliding window catches
Fit wooden battery cover
Fit under-wing sealing plates
Fit Ecurie Safety Fast transfers
Check recommended heater switch fitted
Fit speedometer with trip and magnified apertures
Fit illuminated clocks
Fit Weston revolution counter and illuminate
Fit oil and water pressure and water temperature guage and illuminate
Supply three ignition keys
Supply two boot lid keys
Check instruments and controls
Fit latest type Butler navigation lamp
Check speedometer for accuracy
Fit two-pin plug on near-side parcel shelf
Fit two-pin plug on near-side of the handbrake
Fit driver's demister bar
Fit 700 LHD headlamp units
Fit 494 reversing lamp
Fit theostat switch for driver's instruments
Fit rheostat switch for Smiths clocks

Focus lamps
Fit single-speed wiper motor
Renew wiper blades
Fit headlamp flick switch
Fit plastic covers to headlamps
Fit covers for fog lamps
Fit Duraband tyres and valve caps
Fit stowage for tyre guage and brake adjusting spanner
Stow modified jack
Stow wheel-brace
Change clutch springs to latest type
Check sealing for carburetters
Check sealing for cylinder head
Fit paddings to both door locks
Check driver's and passenger's seat
Check seat belts
Check sun visors
Check stop clocks
Stow spare headlamp bulbs
Fit two fog lamps
Stow two spare wheels
Fit sump guard
Fit latest type shock absorber rubbers
Use castellated nuts and split pins on ball joints
Check sub frames for working loose
Fit air cooling to front brakes
Fit modified rear pivot shafts
Clean car inside and out
Wash and polish, repaint as necessary

The 997 Mini-Cooper

In comparison to the 850, the Mini-Cooper gave such a vast improvement in performance that there was little need for much engine modification from the standard specification. The rally cars produced around 70 bhp, they proved a lot more reliable than the 850s and the same suspension modifications that were proved on the 850 could be applied to the new model. Some experiments were carried out using the 731 camshaft in place of the 948 camshaft and, with a rev limit of 7,000 rev/min, the 948 was preferred as it gave better low-speed torque.

Starting with the 997 Mini-Cooper, Abingdon began to carry out its own engine development programme with Cliff Humphries working in close co-operation with Eddie Maher, Chief of Engines Branch at

Coventry. A more detailed build sheet for the works cars was instituted at this time, as is shown by the following sheet for the car built for Rauno Aaltonen to drive on the 1963 Monte Carlo Rally.

Cylinder block

Bore size	Standard
Fume pipes	Standard
Camshaft	Standard
Crankshaft	Standard, balanced with Deva bush
Flywheel	Standard, balanced
Clutch	Standard, bonded and riveted facings
Release bearings	Standard
Camshaft bearings	Standard
Crankshaft bearings	Standard
Connecting rods	Standard, lined up
Pistons	Standard
Oil pump	Standard Hobourn
Oil pump drive	Standard, latest type
Camshaft gear	Steel
Crankshaft gear	Steel
Timing chain	Reynolds
Core plugs	Standard
Dip stick and washer	Standard
Oil filter element	Standard
Distributor	Model 40819
Ignition setting	5 degs BTC
Engine rubbers	Standard
Engine number plate	Check with log book
Idler gear	Solid
Primary gear	Deva bushed
Oil pressure	Check
Sump and protection	RAF type guard
Sump plug	Standard
Oil cooler	None

Cylinder head

Type	Standard, do not polish
Compression ratio	Check 9 to 1
Combustion space	31·1 cc
Exhaust valves	Standard
Inlet valves	Standard
Top collar	AEA 402
Bottom caps	AEA 403
Valve spring inner	AEA 401
Valve spring outer	AEA 311
Thermostat	74 degs
Exhaust manifold	Match to ports, do not polish
Inlet manifold	Match to ports, do not polish

Plugs	N3
Rocker assembly	Standard

Transmission

Gear ratios	Standard
Gear material	Special EN36B (second gear), rest standard
Type of transmission	Special straight cut
Selector bars and forks	Standard
Gear lever	Fit anti-rattle
Drive shafts	Standard
Differential ratio	4·1 to 1
Clutch adjustment	Standard

Carburetter

Type	Twin 1½ in. SU
Modified	No
Needles	MME
Dash pot springs	Red
Dampers	Standard
Air cleaners	None
Choke cables	MGB type
Heat Shields	None
Heat collecting box	Yes
Induction	Standard
Linkage	Peg and fork type
Accelerator cable	Special nylon insert type
Float level	Fit extensions
Vibration	None

Chassis

Front struts	Standard with packing washers
Rear struts	Standard van type with 0·100 in. washer
Anti-roll bar	None
Wishbones	Standard
Bump rubbers	Standard
Front shock absorbers	Special Armstrong
Rear shock absorbers	Special Armstrong turned down to clear body
Torsion bar	None
Chassis strengthening	None
Chassis modifications	Fit bump rubbers for rear swing arm
Engine mounting brackets	Standard
Shock absorber mounting	Special brackets at front
Bumpers	Remove overriders
Jacking points	Standard
Height of car	Raise to maximum
Front hubs	Overhaul
Rear hubs	Overhaul
Stub axles	Overhaul
Towing eyes	Special U bolts fitted to rear subframe

| Radius arms | Standard |
| Tie rods | Standard |

Cooling System

Fan	Standard 16 blade
Radiator	Standard
Water pump	Standard
Hoses	Check
Fanbelt	Fit stretched and spare
Radiator blind	Fit Moray type
Blanking	Fit muffs
Anti Freeze	Castrol
Radiator cap	Standard
Header tank	None
Temperature gauge	Fit capillary type
Radiator drain plug	Check

Electrics

Dynamo	C40 with cast iron plates
Starter	Standard race tested
Coil	HA12 race tested
Regulator box	RB310 race tested
Battery and fixing	Standard, reverse battery and lengthen cable
Dynamo pulley	Standard
Waterproofing	Silicone grease
Wiper motor	Single speed race tested with special wheel boxes
Wiper motor switch	Standard
Wiper blades and arms	Renew
Headlamps	Special
Headlamp bulbs	White vertical dip
Fog lamps	Pair 700 lamps
Fog lamp switch	One for each lamp
Fog lamp bulbs	White transverse
Long range lamps	One 576 fitted central
Long range switch	Yes
Long range bulb	White axial
Reverse lamp	576 fitted to boot lid
Reverse lamp switch	Special with indicator incorporated
Reverse lamp bulb	Standard white
Tail lamps	Standard
Stop lamps	Standard
Flasher lamps	Standard
Flasher switch	Standard
Two-pin plugs	Fit one to dash panel
Navigator's lamp	Flexible Butler type
Demister bar	One on driver's side
Lamp covers	Fit to all front lamps
Horns	Twin Mixo Minors

Horn buttons   Standard for driver, foot operated for passenger
Panel lights   Switch rheostat type
Panel light rev counter   Standard internal
Panel light speedometer   Standard
Panel light clocks   External
Ammeter   None
Headlamp flick switch   Yes
Brake light switch   None
Tail light switch   None
Screen washer   Electric Tudor
Battery protection   Check terminal rubbers

Steering
Column   Standard
Steering wheel   Wood rim
Steering wheel nut   Check
Rack and pinion   Standard
Steering arms   Standard
Track arms   Standard
Track wheels $\frac{1}{16}$ in. toe out
Camber and castor   Check
Lubricate   All points
Lock nuts   Fit castellated nuts and split pins
Steering ratio   Standard
Adjustment   Check
Line up steering wheel   Yes

Exhaust
System   Competition type
Silencer   Special
Hanging brackets   Standard
Front support bracket   Standard

Petrol system
Tank   Fit twin tanks
Tank fixing   Standard
Fuel guage   Standard
Bumps   Standard with protection
Pipes   Standard
Tank fillers   Quick release
Tank protection   Wood strips for studded tyres
Pipe protection   Cover with metal channels
Leaks   Check
Petrol filters   Check
Tank breather   Check vents in the caps and increase holes

Body
Driver's seat   Microcell
Driver's seat belts   Britax lap strap and diagonal

Passenger's seat	Microcell recliner
Passenger's seat belts	Britax full harness
Windscreen	Laminated
Windscreen washers	Tudor
Sun visors	Standard
Perspex windows	Fit full set
Snow deflector	None
Perspex heat shield	Fit inside windscreen
Rear window wiper	None
Demist	Fit panel to rear window
Heater	Standard
Front and rear wings	Standard
Doors	Standard, check for draughts
Bonnet	Lightened
Bonnet fixings	Fit straps
Safety catches	None
Crash bars	None
Window fixings	Standard
Carpets	Fit full front carpet and secure
Trim	Remove as necessary
Map stowage	Divide passenger's door pocket
Parcel shelf	Standard
Paddings	Fit to doors and locks
Facia	Make and fit special
Switch positions	Arrange as instructed by driver
Registration numbers	Fablon stick on
GB plate	Fablon on rear
Competition numbers	Paint on
Elopress	Fit bracket
Fire extinguisher	Fit bracket
Driving mirror	Standard
Passenger's mirror	Barnacle
Petrol can stowage	None
Kit stowage	As instructed by driver
Spare wheel stowage	Extra clamp for two spares
Scotchlite tape	Rear bumper and door shuts
Grab handles	Fit above passenger's door
Safety Fast emblem	Yes
Union Jacks	Yes
Rally Plates	Prepare for fitting

Controls

Accelerator pedal	Modify for heel and toe
Accelerator pedal brackets	Modify
Acclerator cable	Standard
Brake pedal	Standard
Pedal box	Standard
Clutch pedal	Standard

| Handbrake lever | Modify to fly-off type |
| Handbrake cables | Check quadrant and grease |

Instruments

Speedometer	Special KPH calibrated
Trip instrument	Fit magnifier
Cables	Standard
Clocks	Twin Heuer
Rev counter	Smiths electrical
Safety guages	Fit water temperature and oil pressure
Ignition key	Check number and fit spare
Boot key	Check number and fit spare

Tyres and wheels

Tyres	Four SP Dunlops in car
Tubes	Yes
Spare wheels	Two SP with spikes in boot
Valve caps	Check
Balance	Yes

Brakes

Master cylinder	Standard
Master cylinder mountings	Standard
Wheel cylinders	Standard
Front calipers	Standard
Front pads	DS11
Rear shoes	VG95
Bed brakes and fade	Yes and fade spare set
Pipes	Run inside car and protect where necessary
Fluid	Heavy duty Lockheed
Limiting valve	Standard
Air cooling	None
Servo	None
Waterproofing	Check back plates

Kit

Jack	Modified
Plug carrier	None
Spare coil	None
Wheelbrace	Two modified
Tyre guage	Clip in cockpit
Route card holder	Yes
Chains	Yes
Oil stowage	Yes

The 1071 Mini-Cooper 'S'

The first Cooper 'S' gave as big an advantage over the 997 Cooper as that model did over the 850. The 1071 proved that with only basic conventional tuning, lightening, balancing and careful assembly, it could win outright the rallies of the day.

The works cars produced around 92 bhp but, with a smooth power curve, the standard transmission assemblies were still capable of standing up to hard rally work. The suspension too gave little trouble. The only major modification that came with this model was the replacement of the standard hub bearings with Timkin roller bearings. This latter came into use on the standard production car, as did modified steering arms.

This is the build sheet of the famous 1071 Mini (33 EJB) which Paddy Hopkirk drove to victory in the 1964 Monte Carlo Rally.

Cylinder Block

Bore size	Standard
Fume pipes	Fit two
Camshaft	Standard
Crankshaft	Standard balanced
Flywheel	Special balanced
Clutch	Special diaphram type
Release bearing	Standard
Camshaft bearings	Standard
Crankshaft bearings	Standard
Connecting rods	Standard
Pistons	Standard bore, flat top
Oil pump	Standard
Oil pump drive	Standard
Camshaft gear	Standard
Crankshaft gear	Standard
Timing chain	Standard
Core plugs	Fit retainers
Dip stick and washer	Blue dip stick end
Oil filter element	Standard
Distributor	Race tested
Ignition setting	7 degs BTDC
Engine rubbers	Standard
Engine plate	Check with log book
Idler gear	Standard
Primary gear	Standard
Oil pressure	Check (80 lb)
Sump and protection	RAF type sump guard
Sump plug	Standard
Oil cooler	MGB type with special flex pipes wire locked

Cylinder head

Type	Standard cleaned only
Compression ratio	Maximum given with pistons 10·5 to 1

Combustion space	Check (21·3 cc)
Exhaust valves	Standard
Inlet valves	Standard
Top caps	Standard marked W
Bottom caps	AEA 654
Valve spring inner	AEA 652
Valve spring outer	AEA 524
Thermostat	Fit wax type
Sealing points	Fit bracket as instructed
Exhaust manifold	Standard
Inlet manifold	Standard
Plugs	Champion N4
Rocker assembly	Standard

Transmission

Gear ratios	Standard
Gear material	Standard
Type of transmission	Spur cut gears
Selector bars and forks	Tighten
Gear lever	Check for rattle and easy movement
Drive shafts	Standard
Differential ratio	4·1 to 1
Clutch adjustment	Standard

Carburetters

Type	Twin 1½ in. SU
Modified	Fit float chamber extensions
Needles	MME
Dashpot springs	Red
Dampers	0·070 in.
Air cleaners	None, fit trumpets
Choke cables	Standard
Heat shields	None
Heat collecting box	Yes
Induction	Standard
Linkage	Fork and peg
Accelerator cable	Nylon insert, special check on alignment
Float level	Check with extensions
Vibration	Special check

Chassis

Front cones	Standard
Rear cones	Standard
Front struts	Standard
Rear struts	Standard
Anti roll bars	None
Wishbones	Standard
Bump rubbers	Fit extra to rear
Front shock absorbers	Special competition

Rear shock absorbers	Special competition, turn down the tops
Chassis modification	None
Engine mounting brackets	Standard
Shock absorber mounting	Fit special brackets to the front
Bumpers	Standard
Jacking points	Standard
Height of car	Standard
Front hubs	Standard, overhaul
Rear hubs	Standard, overhaul
Stub axles	Standard
Towing eyes	Front and rear
Overriders	Standard
Radius arms	Standard
Tie rods	Split pin nuts

Cooling system

Type of fan	Four bladed
Type of radiator	16 gills per inch
Water pump	Standard
Hoses	Standard
Fanbelt	Special and fit spare to engine
Radiator blind	None
Blanking	Blank off half off-side and fit muffs
Anti freeze	Yes
Radiator cap	13 lb/in^2
Header tank	Standard
Temperature gauge	Standard
Radiator drain plug	Wire lock
Flush system	Yes

Electrics

Dynamo	C40-22746 28 amp with bearings
Starter	Standard race tested
Coil	HA12
Regulator box	To suit dynamo
Battery and fixing	Standard battery turned round with larger terminal covers and insulate
Dynamo pulley	AEA 535 large
Water proofing	Maximum
Wiper motor	Twin speed maximum wipe, not wired through ignition
Wiper motor switch	Twin speed
Wiper blades and arms	Standard
Headlamps	Special fitted with iodine bulbs
Headlamp bulbs	Iodine with dip to two 576 fog lamps
Fog lamps	Two 700 latest type
Fog lamp switch	One for each lamp
Fog lamp bulbs	White

Long range lamps	One 576 fitted central
Long range switch	Three position wired with main beam
Long range bulb	White axial
Reverse lamp	One 576 fitted to boot lid
Reverse lamp switch	Special with indicator
Reverse lamp bulb	White transverse
Tail lamps	Standard
Stop lamps	Standard
Flasher lamps	Standard
Flasher switch	Standard
Two pin plug	One fitted to facia
Navigator's lamp	Flexible Butlers type
Demister bars	None
Lamp covers	All front lamps
Horns	Twin Mixo Minors
Horn buttons	Standard for driver, foot button for passenger
Panel lights	Standard
Light for rev counter	Standard
Panel light for speedometer	Standard
Panel light for odometer	Special
Panel light for clocks	External
Ammeter	None
Headlamp flick switch	Yes
Brake light switch	None
Tail light switch	None
Screen washer	Tudor electrical
Headlamp washers	Tudor electrical
Starter switch	Fit push button control
Roof lamp	Fit one with 700 iodine bulb

Steering

Column	Standard and check bottom clamp bolt
Steering wheel	Wood rim
Steering wheel nut	Tighten and check
Rack and pinion	Standard
Steering arms	Standard
Track arms	Split pin nuts
Track wheels	$\frac{1}{8}$ in. toe out
Camber and castor	Check
Lock nuts	Fit castellated nuts and split pins
Steering ratio	Standard
Adjustment	Check
Line up steering wheel	Yes

Exhaust

Type of system	Special competition latest type
Type of silencer	Special competition latest type
Hanging brackets	Special
Support bracket at front	Special

Petrol system

Tank	Fit twin tanks
Tank fixing	Standard
Fuel guage	Standard
Pumps	Fit twin pumps with protection
Pipes	Cover where necessary
Tank fillers	Quick release
Tank protection	Yes, both tanks
Pipe protection	Yes
Heat protection	None
Petrol filters	Check and clean
Tank breather	Check hole in caps

Body

Driver's seat	Microcell
Passenger's seat	Microcell recliner
Seat belts	To be specified by crew
Windscreen	Laminated heated Triplex
Windscreen washer	Tudor with de-icing fluid
Sun visors	Standard
Perspex windows	Yes, side and rear
Snow deflector	None
Perspex heater shield	Yes, inside windscreen
Rear window wiper	None
Demist	Modify ducts as instructed
Heater	Latest type
Front wings	Standard, modify for lamps
Rear wings	Standard
Doors	Standard, check for draughts
Panels	Standard
Bonnet	Standard
Bonnet fixing	Fit safety strap
Safety catches	None
Crash bar	None
Window fixings	Standard
Carpet	Fit full front
Trim	Remove as necessary
Map stowage	Divide near-side door pocket
Parcel shelf	None
Padding	Fit to doors and locks
Facia	Special
Switch positions	Arrange as instructed
Registration numbers	Fablon stick on
GB plate	Fablon stick on
Competition numbers	Painted
Eolopress	Fit one
Fire extinguisher	Fit one
Driving mirror	Standard for driver, Barnacle for passenger

Petrol can stowage	None
Spare wheel stowage	For two spiked tyres
Scotchlite tape	Rear bumper and door shuts
Grab handle	Above passenger's door
Safety fast emblem	Yes
Union Jacks	Yes
Rally plates	Prepare for fitting

Controls

Accelerator pedal	Modify for heel-and-toe
Accelerator pedal brackets	Modify
Accelerator cable	Nylon insert type
Accelerator linkage	Fork and peg
Brake pedal	Standard
Pedal box	Standard
Clutch pedal	Standard
Handbrake	Modify to fly-off

Instruments

Speedometer	KPH special
Trip instrument	Halda with magnifier
Cables	Halda specials and check reduction box screw
Clocks	Pair Heuer
Rev counter	Smiths electric
Safety guage	Yes, water and oil
Ignition key	Check number and mount spare
Boot key	Check number and mount spare

Tyres and wheels

Type of tyre	To be decided after recce
Tubes	Yes
Spare wheels	Two spikes
Valve caps	Yes
Balance	Yes

Brakes

Master cylinder	Standard
Master cylinder mountings	Standard
Rear wheel cylinders	Standard
Front wheel cylinders	Standard
Front calipers	Standard
Front pads	DS11
Rear shoes	VG95
Bed brakes and fade	Yes, with spare set pads
Pipes	Cover as necessary, run main inside body
Fluid	Disc brake heavy duty
Limiting valve	Standard
Servo	Move to inside the car on passenger's side
Waterproofing	Yes

Kit

Jack	M G B modified type
Wheel brace	Pair stowed
Tyre guage	Yes, clip on facia
Route card holder	Yes
Crash helmet stowage	Yes
Chains	Yes
Oil stowage	Yes

The 1275 Mini-Cooper 'S'

With the introduction of the 1275 Mini-Cooper 'S', a lot more engine and transmission development work was carried out at Abingdon. The Competitions Department now had the use of the engine test beds of the M G Development Department and a rolling road was also available. Considerable liaison work started with Daniel Richmond at Downton Engineering and with John Cooper and Ginger Devlin at the Cooper Car Company. Eddie Maher and Derek Frost at Engines Branch maintained a close watch on all that went on. On the transmission side there was considerable co-operation from Harry Gardner at Longbridge and Jimmy Cockrell at Tractors and Transmission Branch.

The competition development of the 1275 is best documented by reference to each major component in turn. The early 1275 cars ran with standard cylinder heads mildly polished and gas flowed by the Abingdon mechanics. Later, heads were purchased from Downton Engineering and these were used on all Group 2 cars, basically without any further development throughout the full period of the 1275 competitions. The larger valve heads by Janspeed Engineering were tried on later Group 6 cars, and for rallycross, but these were found to offer only minimal advantages.

As a direct result of experience in competitions (racing rather than rallying in this case) cylinder blocks with strengthened centre main bearings were later introduced; also a stronger flange between the crankcase and gearbox.

The 148 camshaft was used on early cars, then the 648 camshaft became most popular for Group 2. The 510 camshaft, designed principally for the 1966 Monte (Group 1), gave smoother torque and a slight increase in valve crash. This camshaft which became the standard 'S' type camshaft, was favoured by some drivers, particularly on forestry stages, for it gave much improved low down flexibility which saved wear and tear on transmissions in the lower speed range.

Standard inlet manifolds were used for Group 2 with twin H4 1½ in. SU carburetters which gave about 90 bhp. A further 7 bhp, improved torque and acceleration, was later gained by using the twin special split Webers, tried for the first time with some dramas on the 1968 Monte (see chapter 12).

The rocker gear on early 1275s was used in its standard form but later lightened gear was used which incorporated eccentric rocker bushes to increase the lift. This was found to be as effective as a camshaft change.

Overheating problems with the 1275 were generally caused by piston failures. Early cars, fitted with standard pistons, gave troubles with the piston ring lands cracking and the gudgeon pins tightening up. This was partially cured by increasing the gudgeon pin clearance and by reducing the number of compression rings from three to two, thus increasing the width of the land. Piston ovality was also increased so that the gudgeon pin was less likely to come into contact with the cylinder wall. Later, forged pistons were used which had the advantage of staying in one piece if they did crack. (Fred Cockcroft of Hepworth & Grandage contributed a lot to solving the Mini's piston troubles.) To further assist with the overheating problem, an increased capacity impeller was fitted to the water pump and this item was subsequently put into production on the standard car.

The standard nitrided crankshaft gave little trouble and the 1275 must have one of the strongest crankshafts of any production engine. The standard connecting rods, crack tested and balanced, also proved quite adequate, as did steel flywheels – even when they were excessively lightened.

On the transmission side, the diaphragm-spring clutch with an increased rating was used with the standard centre plate and lining bonded and riveted. Standard material crack-tested drive shafts gave little trouble but the early rubber couplings were replaced by the Hardy Spicer steel coupling from the 1966 Monte onwards. This modification was also adopted on the standard car. Early cars ran with standard gearboxes but later close-ratio spur-cut gears in special material were introduced.

The cone rubber suspension of the early cars was modified only with the use of competition shock absorbers. With the introduction of hydrolastic suspension, higher rate front and rear units were used.

Later front shock absorbers were homologated in Group 2 along with adjustable front tie rods. For circuit racing a rear anti-roll bar was favoured on the hydrolastic cars but not on the cone rubber suspension cars. Aeon bump rubbers were also fitted at the rear.

Other items which were introduced on to the production car or homologated in Group 2 included the wider $4\frac{1}{2}$ in. wheels, an oil cooler, twin fuel tanks, limited slip differential, an improved gearbox mounting kit, perspex windows and lightweight panels.

The current (as of January 1971) FIA homologation form for the 1275 Mini-Cooper 'S' is reproduced in the Appendix. The following is the build sheet for the car driven by Tony Fall on the 1968 Monte.

Cylinder block

Block	Latest strengthened type
Bore size	Plus 0·020 in.
Modifications	Machine the face to 0·010 in. off the piston crown
Fume pipes	One standard with long hose. Blank off the clack valve and cut holes in the hose
Camshaft	AEA 648
Crankshaft	Balanced, double drilled and blanked off
Flywheel	Steel, extra lightened and balanced
Clutch	Diaphragm (orange) balanced
Release bearing	Standard, repack with HMP grease
Bearings cam	Standard
Bearings crank	Special Vandervell
Connecting rods	Standard, line up and balance. Machine a groove in the rod stretch bolts (0·003 in.)
Pistons	Forged (plus 0·020 in.) ovalized with 450 pad rings
Oil pump	Standard concentric, strip and clean rough casting
Oil pump drive	Standard
Camshaft gear	Machine to line up and tighten
Crankshaft gear	Standard, machine to line up and tighten
Timing chain	Standard
Core plugs	Peen around the edges
Dip stick and washer	Blue the dipstick and check the length
Oil filter element	Standard
Distributor	40979B with latest condensor and rotor arm grease point pivot
Ignition setting	Test on rolling road and report
Engine rubbers	Latest standard rubbers
Engine number plate	Check with log book
Idler gear	Standard helical, EN 355 material

Primary Gear	Special, Vandervell steel back bush, helical in EN 355 material
Oil pressure	Check and report
Sump and protection	Standard guard
Sump plug	Standard
Oil cooler	ARO 9809 with special flex pipes, check for fouling
	Modify oil cooler mounting and the front steady bracket to clear the alternator
Engine steady bracket	Modify the bush at the bulkhead end. Fit a spacer and a bolt for easy removal

Cylinder head

Type	Downton
Modified	Check for six brass plugs
Compression ratio	12·6:1
Amount removed	Downton specification
Combustion space	16·4 cc
Exhaust valves	Standard
Inlet valves	Standard
Top caps	Marked W
Bottom caps	AEA 403
Valve spring inner	AEA 652, check pressure
Valve spring outer	AEA 524, check pressure
Thermostate	Standard. Do not blank off bypass
Sealing points	None
Exhaust manifold	Downton
Inlet manifold	Downton
Plugs	Champion N60Y
Rocker assembly	Fit latest type. Remove 0·055 in. from the pillars. Fit modified shaft, drill and countersink plain pillar for oilway. Line up rocker arm with valve stem

Transmission

Gear ratios	Close ratio
Gear material	Special crack tested
Type of transmission	Spur cut gears
Sump plug	Standard
Selector bars and forks	Check and tighten
Filler cap modifications	Check and drill holes in the slot of the filler cap and one $\frac{3}{8}$-in. hole in the middle
Gear lever	Standard, check ease of change
Drive shafts	Special latest modified type from Hardy Spicer with needle roller bearings
Differential ratio	4·2:1
Clutch adjustment	Standard

Oil pick up pipe	Fit modified type
Remote control mounting	Fit Michell type rubbers

Carburetters

Type	Twin split Webers
Air cleaners	Fit stub pipes, less breathers
Choke cables	Standard
Heat shields	Fit asbestos to bulkhead under the bonnet
Heat collecting box	Make and fit
Induction	Downton
Linkage	Fork and peg, line up
Accelerator cable	Special Smiths nylon insert
Vibration	Wire lock banjo bolts to the float chamber bolts

Chassis

Displacer units	Double blue rear, single blue front. Fit double locating bracket at front
Rear struts	Standard, orange (30 lb) helper spring and split pin the bottom pin
Anti roll bar	None
Wishbones	Standard, fit standard rubbers latest type
Bump rubbers	Aeon
Engine mounting brackets	Standard
Bumpers	Standard
Jacking points	Quick lift brackets, front and rear
Ride height	Standard, approximately 13 in. from wheel centre to wheel arch
Front hubs	Standard, checked and packed with FCB grease
Rear hubs	Special Timkin with FCB grease
Stub axles	Standard
Towing eyes	Two at front
Overriders	None
Radius arms	Standard
Tie rods	Split pin nuts and fit new rubbers. Fit skid shields
Fog lamp brackets	Fit quick release type
Mud flaps	Front and rear

Cooling system

Radiator	Type DEV 3023 and bolt bottom end solid
Type of fan	Fit four bladed with machined ends
Radiator capacity	16 gills per inch with $\frac{1}{4}$ in.-fixing screws
Water pump	Standard small pulley
Hoses	Standard
Fan belt	Goodyear special 1304 H and fit spare
Radiator blind	Fit muff to the grille
Blanking	None

Anti freeze	Yes
Radiator cap	13 lb wire on
Header tank	Standard with expansion tank
Temperature gauge	Special Smiths capillary tube
Radiator drain plug	Wire lock

Electrics

Alternator	Modify earth wire
Starter	Standard RT 25110 wired with solenoid and push button
Coil	HA 12 with water proofing
Regulator box	For alternator 4 TR 37423A
Battery and fixing	Special type fitted with terminals away from the petrol tank
Alternator pulley	AEA 535
Waterproofing	Silicone grease, rubber covers on coil and distributor with alloy plate in front
Front auxiliary lamps	Fit five-way connectors for quick removal
Wiper motor	Two speed
Wiper motor switch	Two speed to driver's and navigator's panel
Wiper blades and arms	Standard with deep-throated wheel boxes
Headlamps	European E4 (white)
Headlamp bulbs	Vertical dip 80–60
Fog lamps	Two 700 latest type fitted with iodine bulbs
Fog lamp switch	One for each light mounted adjacent
Fog lamp bulbs	Iodine
Long range lamps	Fit two centre with headlamp units
Long range switch	One for each light mounted adjacent
Long range bulb	Iodine
Reverse lamp	576 with 21 watt bulb
Reverse lamp switch	Mechanical fitting to gearbox
Tail lamps	Standard
Stop lamps	Standard
Flasher lamps	Standard position incorporated with side lamp
Flasher switch	Standard
Two pin plugs	One in navigator's glove pocket
Navigator's lamp	Butlers flex type in the glove pocket
Demister bars	None
Lamp covers	All front lamps
Horns	Maserati
Horn buttons	Standard for driver, foot operated for navigator
Panel lights	Standard
Panel light for clocks	Four external
Ammeter	None
Head lamp flick switch	Standard
Battery	Make and fit cover and supply bolt on protection
Battery cable	Fit large type terminal covers to insulate and run inside the car

Screen washer	Tudor electric. Fit switch to driver's and navigator's panel. Fit special Tudor chrome jets (0·040 in.)
Headlamp washers	Specials
Cigar lighter	Standard, on driver's side

Steering

Type of column	Standard, check bottom clamp bolt and tighten
Steering wheel	Leather covered with thumb pads and matt black spokes
Steering wheel nut	Tighten
Rack and pinion	Special, latest type. Fit modified U bolt to location on the side of the rack
Steering arms	Standard, latest type, strip and clean lap faces
Track arms	Standard, split pin nuts and check taper fit
Camber and castor	Check
Lock nuts	Fit castellated nuts and split pin both ends of the rods
Steering ratio	Standard
Steering adjustment	Check and line up steering wheel
Track wheels	$\frac{1}{8}$ in. toe out
Ball pins	Fit special, BTA 445

Exhaust

System	Fit skid under the silencer and turn the end up
Silencer	Competition
Hanging brackets	Drill special rubbers and fit bolt
Front support bracket	Special and fit steel exhaust clips in place of Jubilee clips and weld on

Petrol system

Tank	Fit twin and wire up rear connection
Tank fixing	Standard
Fuel gauge	Standard with bi-metal strip
Pumps	Fit twin pumps under the rear seat but wire one only
Pipes	Run inside car
Tank fillers	Standard, wire on
Tank protection	Asbestos shield. Mould in sharp edges with Isopon
Pipe protection	Inside cars where necessary
Petrol filters	Standard, clean
Tank breather	Fit standard pipes and check outlets are clear

Body

Driver's seat	Special, fibreglass
Driver's harness	Special Irvin lap and diagonal snap in fixing

Passenger's harness	Special Irvin full harness
Passenger's seat	Special recliner, fit straps for harness
Windscreen	Laminated Triplex electric
Windscreen washer	Tudor electric, fit two nozzles to driver's side
Sun visor	Standard, latest type
Demist	Fit rear Clearview as high as possible
Heater	Standard
Front wings	Standard with wheel spats, pop rivet finisher
Rear wings	Standard with wheel spats, pop rivet finisher
Doors	Standard with plastic finisher inside
Panels	All standard
Bonnet fixings	Standard, fit safety straps
Crash bar	Fit Aley type
Carpets	Insulated with asbestos blanket under front
Trim	Standard
Map stowage	Divide nearside door pocket
Parcel shelf	None
Door draughts	Check, crews are complaining of this
Water test	Check and rectify
Paddings	Fit to door pocket, locks and pillars
Facia	Special made by Competitions, matt black all chrome
Switch positions	Arrange as instructed
Intercom	Fit to crash bar
Remote control	Make up and fit emergency strap
Registration plates	Stick on front, number plate rear
GB plate	Fablon
Competition numbers	Paint matt black on white patch
Eolopress	Fit one
Fire extinguisher	Fit one
Driving mirror	Latest Mini type with large arm and dip
Passenger's mirror	Barnacle type
Petrol can stowage	None
Kit stowage	Check with crew
Scotchlite tape	Rear bumpers and door shuts
Grab handles	Fit one above passenger's door
Rally plates	Prepare for fixing
Crew names	Latest stick on type

Controls

Accelerator pedal	Modify for heel-and-toe
Accelerator pedal brackets	Standard
Accelerator cable	Nylon insert Smiths type
Accelerator linkage	Fork and peg
Brake pedal	Standard
Pedal box	Standard
Clutch pedal	Standard

| Handbrake lever | Modify for fly-off type |
| Handbrake cables | Grease well, use PBC on quadrant and pivots |

Instruments

Speedometer	KPH with trip
Trip instrument	Halda Twinmaster with windows removed and taped
Cables	Halda special
Clocks	Twin Heuer
Rev counter	Smiths electric
Safety gauge	Yes
Ignition key	Fit spare

Tyres and wheels

Tyres	As instructed after tyre tests
Tubes	Yes
Spare wheels	Roof rack with four, two in boot
Valve caps	Yes
Balance	Yes
Wheels	Minilite

Brakes

Master cylinder	Standard 'S' type
Master cylinder mountings	Standard
Rear wheel cylinder	Special checked with threaded boss
Front calipers	Standard with heat pads
Front pads	DS 11
Rear shoes	VG95/1
Bed brakes and fade	As many sets as possible
Pipes	Run inside car
Fluid	Lockheed disc
Limiting valve	Fit 450 lb/in^2
Servo	Standard
Water proofing	Maximum
Protection	Re-run the rear brake pipes behind the brake cables and make up a shield and fit special front flex pipes

Kit

Jack	Quick action, stow upright behind driver's seat
Wheel brace	Two, spinner type
Bulbs	One box
Tyre gauge	One, clip on door
Route card holder	Yes
Helmet stowage	Yes
Oil stowage	One can
Pencil holder	On passenger's side

CHAPTER 8

PROTEST YEAR

International rallying, like so many sports, has its ups and downs, its good years and its bad. 1966 has gone down in the record books as the year rallying hit the headlines, but the year every rallyist would like to forget – the year of protests and disqualifications. And, of course, it all started with the Monte.

A lot has been written about the Monte fiasco but nowhere was the background to the true story of the events that led up to the famous disqualification of the three 'winning' Minis better told than by Stuart Turner and BMC's Competitions Press Officer, Wilson McComb, in *Safety Fast* magazine. Much of the following account is taken from their story.

The trouble really started in June 1965 when the FIA published the general rally regulations (known as Appendix J) for all events in 1966. This included definitions of different categories of cars and listed the modifications permitted in each category together with the numbers of production cars that had to be made to qualify for each category. In previous years there was the additional requirement that 1,000 identical cars had to have been built in 12 consecutive months to qualify for Group I or Group II but only 100 were required for Group III. The details of these regulations ran to several pages of small print. The only significant change that appeared in the 1966 Appendix J was that the Group I production requirement was now 5,000 units, Group II was still 1,000 and Group III raised to 500. This did not at first cause concern because the 1275 Mini-Cooper 'S' entries had always run in Groups II or III trim.

However, the big surprise came when the Monte Carlo Rally regulations were issued in November. The Monte had in recent years been run on some kind of handicap basis, designed ostensibly to give a fair and equal chance of victory to any kind of car. This year it was immediately apparent that only a Group I car would stand a chance of winning at all. Group II and III cars would run under such severe handicaps that it would have been a waste of time entering cars in these categories.

Looking at it in retrospect it was quite obvious that the Monegasque were fed up with these little foreign cars winning 'their' Rally outright twice in succession and were determined that they should not do it a third time. They were convinced that 5,000 Mini-Cooper 'S's' could not possibly have been built in the previous 12 months; and they believed that a virtually standard Mini-Cooper 'S' could not possibly win the Rally.

The regulations were late in being issued anyway, and the closing date for entries was uncomfortably near. Both Appendix J and the Rally regulations were full of ambiguities and the team managers for all the major manufacturers ran round in small circles trying to find out for certain if the cars they wanted to use would, in fact, be eligible to run. Volvo and Saab, who had been regular competitors for many years, gave up the problem as insoluble in the time available and decided not to enter the Monte that year at all.

Stuart Turner believed that he could sort this one out and the entries were made. What the Rally organizers did not realize was that successful rallying sells cars and the year's production figure for the Mini-Cooper 'S' had already stood at just under 5,000. By stepping up production just a little, 5,047 identical cars were built within the specified 12 months and the model was homologated as a Group I car. The details of exactly what modifications were permitted were still far from clear in many respects, particularly as no less than three revised versions of Appendix J were issued by the FIA during the last few weeks before the Monte.

In December Stuart Turner and Henry Taylor (then Competitions Manager of Ford, who was in a similar position) flew to Paris to try and sort out the matter with the FIA, taking with them a questionnaire of over 100 points that were not clear to them. They returned satisfied that their cars complied with the regulations in every respect. It is significant that the matter of headlamp modification did not appear on this questionnaire, for this was one matter about which there appeared to be no doubt whatsoever.

It was obvious that the regulations were going to be strictly enforced this year and that the Group I regulations were stricter than usual anyway. There was far too much at stake for either team to take the slightest risk of infringing the regulations in any way, and when the cars were eventually prepared both team managers sincerely believed that their cars were 100 per cent in accordance with both the word and the spirit of the regulations. B M C at least dared not do otherwise. They were setting out with the intention of winning the Monte – and the winning cars are always fully scrutineered.

Even so, never before had they had so little time in which to prepare cars for the Monte and never before has the preparation been carried out under such difficulties. The specification of the cars had to be changed three times as revised versions of Appendix J were issued with changes to the permitted modifications and in fact the final version was not received at Abingdon until after Paddy Hopkirk's car had been sent on its way to the Warsaw start!

When Wilson McComb arrived in Monte Carlo before the start and went to Rally Headquarters he was immediately button-holed by a senior official and asked to arrange for B M C mechanics to be standing by when scrutineering after the Rally took place, for they would be needed should the scrutineers wish the cars to be completely dismantled for inspection. This is a reasonable request, but the manner of making it showed that scrutineering was uppermost in the organizers' minds as far as the B M C cars were concerned. Furthermore, it soon became apparent that there was an atmosphere of real hostility towards the British team, both from the Rally officials and the French press. In the latter's sports pages there was much talk about unnamed 'cheats'. 'The cheats have had their day . . . The cheats will be exposed' and so on. The pro-British manager of a Monaco restaurant, where the team members dined before the start, said: 'Ah, messieurs, I regret that you will not win this year: victory will go to . . . (a French car) – it is arranged. . . .'

Allowing for a certain amount of local partisanship and even exaggeration, it seemed obvious that they were gunning for the B M C team. The consciences of the B M C team were as white as the snow on the mountains above Monaco, but down in the town the atmosphere was unpleasant, to say the least.

So the Rally began and the first section – the converging run from the various starting points to Monte Carlo – passed without much incident and no loss of road marks for most competitors. The second section was the start of the really serious stuff: a 24-hour mountain circuit of some 900 miles, with six special timed stages on closed roads for all competitors out from Monte to Chambéry and back again.

Timo Makinen who had started as No. 2, was soon leading on the road but he had some frightening experiences. On the Col de Granier, which was supposed to be closed to traffic, he found that in fact it had not been cleared and that non-competing cars were still using it. He had to do the whole climb with the horns blaring and was unable safely to use the whole road. When he reached the end of the timed section the marshals were not ready for him and he was delayed for some time before being clocked in. Similarly, at the top of the Mount Ventoux hill climb, there was no control to be seen at the end and Timo and co-driver Paul Easter had to drag the marshals out of a near-by cafe before getting their card time stamped!

In spite of these needless delays, at the end of this section Timo was clearly in the lead, followed by Rauno Aaltonen, Roger Clark (Lotus-Cortina), Bengt Soderstrom (Lotus Cortina), and Paddy Hopkirk. The French press in particular were amazed at Timo's performance on the special stages, on several of which he had been fastest *on scratch* out of the entire entry – the hottest Group III sports cars included. They were so amazed, in fact, that they frankly disbelieved that such a performance was possible with a genuine Group I car. Hostility towards B M C increased and thinly veiled hints reflecting deep suspicion flew about.

Then a notice was posted at Rally Headquarters suggesting that some cars might not be complying with the international highway regulations (not the Rally regulations, be it noted) in respect of their headlight-dipping system. A special scrutineering session was arranged for the next morning and all cars were checked by the scarcely scientific method of holding a white cardboard hatbox in front of each car and observing the light pattern on main and dipped beams.

As a result of this a curious notice was posted to the effect that all cars had to have a driving beam and a passing beam and that the following cars had the following arrangements. There followed a list of all the British cars that were subsequently disqualified, with a description of the dipping system in each case. It then said that the acceptability of these dipping arrangements would be decided at final scrutineering: no more than that.

With this vague but worrying pronouncement hanging over them, the top 60 crews set off on the final section of the Rally – an 11 hour run at night, over some 380 miles of mountain roads with six special stages included. As in the previous tests, Timo put up a magnificent performance and by the unofficial reckoning of the press afterwards (subsequently confirmed) he had won outright, with Rauno second, while Paddy had beaten Roger Clark and Bengt Soderstrom into third place.

So to the final scrutineering – and the B M C cars were subjected to a technical inspection that lasted for eight hours! The power units were stripped completely to the last nut and bolt and measured in every dimension. The parts were even weighed as well, with a pair of bathroom scales bought at a local hardware shop – scarcely a precision instrument! Combustion chamber spaces were measured for volume, suspension parts checked, and even the wheels detyred and weighed. Dynamos were checked for standard output and nothing at all could be found to be at variance with the homologated specification, even though their measuring methods were crude in the extreme.

Several times the scrutineers claimed to have found discrepancies, and B M C mechanics had to point out that they were measuring things the wrong way. Once, the scrutineers announced that the combustion chambers were the wrong volume, and they were found to be referring to an homologation form for an 850 Mini instead of 1275. Finally they declared that the front wheel track of Paddy's car was wider than it should be by the monstrous amount of $3\frac{1}{2}$ millimetres! This discovery was released to the French press who crowed with delight at this 'victory for truth'. When it was pointed out that a rubber-suspended car was bound to settle a little in the course of a tough 3,000 mile rally and that the track measurement was meaningless unless related to the ground clearance, they were persuaded to measure again and found that at the declared ground clearance the track was the declared width. The organizers therefore issued a very grudging statement, withdrawing the allegation, without any apology. The matter of the lights had not been raised again since the special inspection of them.

However, when the results were announced, the British contingent were appalled to see that the four top names were simply not there, and that first place had gone to a Citroen. No reason was given for their absence for nearly an hour, when an announcement was made that they had all been disqualified because the lights did not conform to Appendix J (not, be it noted, to international highway law, as before).

No less than 32 formal protests were immediately lodged with the organizers and the battle was on. The protests were rejected and appeals lodged with the A C de Monaco. These were rejected too, and the protests were finally re-submitted to the FIA as the international governing body. All rejected the protest.

It was quite obvious that the organizers themselves had no great confidence in the matter of the lights as grounds for disqualification. Stuart Turner believed them to be entirely acceptable; but even if they were not, it is a minor technical anomaly of no importance whatever to the performance of the cars. The organizers were obviously quite certain that no standard Mini-Cooper 'S' could possibly 'beat the pants off' every other European car, and that thorough scrutineering would soon reveal how the 'cheats' had made them go so fast.

Their chagrin at finding no trace of cheating at all must have been great, particularly in view of their widely publicized suspicions before the event. To save face they had to find something – anything – however trivial and irrelevant. If one really wanted to disqualify any car in any rally, it would almost certainly be possible to find some minor anomoly in every single entry, however honestly and carefully it had been prepared.

The fact that the organizers had constantly to change their attack from one complaint to another suggested firm determination to find *something* wrong. As B M C countered each complaint, they switched to something else. If they had been really sure about the matter of the lights the Minis could have been disqualified before they even set off at all on the exhausting and dangerous last-night section of the Rally, let alone gone through the farce of scrutineering.

The French press were even more hostile by this time. 'This *proved* that the English were cheats,' they said. 'What a victory for *la verité*. While we are told that the headlamps of the British cars were not in accordance with the regulations, who can doubt that in fact they infringed them in many other ways as well? Can we believe that the ordinary car bought from the dealer can be anything like the cars used by Makinen, Aaltonen and Hopkirk?'

The answer to this was to mount an exercise with the co-operation of the French sports paper *l'Équipe* (one that had been consistently critical and suspicious). A completely standard demonstration Mini-Cooper 'S' was borrowed from the local B M C dealer's showroom and matched, up a severe hill climb course chosen by *l'Équipe,* with Paddy's rally car. Both cars were driven up the hill against the watch, alternately by Timo and Alain Bertaut of *l'Action Automobile* and *Moteur* – a French journalist with considerable racing experience.

In this test both Bertaut and Timo put up better times in the showroom car than in the Rally car thus showing, once and for all, that in all important respects the cars that really won that Monte Carlo Rally were genuinely the same as you can buy.

The only victory that the French press could claim was not one for truth, but rather that of prejudice, spite and envy. True enough, B M C got a whole lot more publicity by the disqualification than by winning. And the reception upon the team's return home was some consolation for the drivers' genuine disappointment, not only at losing, but at failing to take home the financial rewards of rallying's richest prize fund. But the organizers' attitude was typified when they even refused to give the crews a finishing plaque to add to their collection!

Flowers troubles

For what was hoped would be a little light relief after the Monte fiasco, Timo Makinen and Rauno Aaltonen were dispatched to Scandinavia to see how they fared on the Swedish Rally. But it was a fruitless effort, Rauno retiring early on when a big rock smashed the radiator against the fan and the boiling engine finally seized. Timo dropped out later when in the lead with a broken drive shaft.

While the Finns were in Sweden, Paddy Hopkirk and Tony Fall fared no better on the Italian Flowers Rally, the event that produced the second international rumpus of 1966. Paddy's stage times were very competitive in the Group II car but an unlucky succession of punctures and an overheating engine finally dropped him way down the leader board.

Tony Fall in a Group I car got no farther than the end of the run-in sections when he was disqualified for having removed the paper air cleaner element to the carburetters as a temporary adjustment to the mixture. The element was in fact being carried in the car but the officials refused to let him continue.

But the most publicized incident of the Rally was the final exclusion of the winning Vic Elford Lotus-Cortina which was thrown out at scrutineering because there was a discrepancy between the number of teeth counted on one of the gears and the total listed on the homologation form (subsequently proved to be a misprint). Another much publicized and highly unsatisfactory end to an international rally.

Three in a row

With disastrous Monte, Swedish and Flowers rallies behind them,

1966 was turning out to be a grim year. But in typical fashion, defeat and disqualification spurred the team on to even greater efforts and the next three events on the programme brought three worthy victories.

On his third drive for the team, Tony Fall gained his spurs in fine style to win the Circuit of Ireland after a superb battle with the works Lotus-Cortinas of Vic Elford, Brian Melia and Roger Clark. Paddy, for a change, did not win 'his' event.

The Finns had a dominating run on the Tulip Rally having tossed before the start to decide who would drive Group I and Group II. Aaltonen claimed the Group II car and won outright from Vic Elford's Cortina, while Makinen won the Group I category from Bengt Soderstrom's Cortina. To round off a very successful trip to Holland, the Minis won the Team Prize along with private entrant Bob Freeborough.

Then Hopkirk and Fall went off to do the Austrian Alpine and this time Paddy made no mistake to win by a clear margin against little opposition. Tony was not so fortunate and hit a pile of logs on a stage which damaged his steering beyond repair.

Everyone was now on top form for an all-out attack on the Acropolis but it seemed that others were still equally determined to put a stop to the run of Mini wins.

Acropolis protests

But for the rumpus at the finish, the 1966 Acropolis could well have been claimed as one of the most sporting events on the calendar. Just about every rally-minded manufacturer sent works teams to Greece, except Citroen who declared that the event was too rough!

From the start under the shadow of the famous Acropolis itself, the 105 crews set off into the rough and very soon it was evident that this was to be a Ford versus B M C affair, the Abingdon Minis of Hopkirk, Makinen and Aaltonen against the Cortinas of Elford, Clark and Soderstrom. Stage time placings gave the advantage first to one team and then the other but the rough going and the keen competition soon took its toll.

Timo clouted a rock and sheared a trailing link bracket, then Elford lost his gears and a lot of time. Rauno dropped out with engine trouble leaving Paddy to battle alone against the Fords. And the lone Mini did just that, finishing a clear leader over the Cortinas of Soderstrom and Clark.

Everyone seemed delighted with the result, with the possible exception of Fords. Cameras clicked as a delighted Paddy with co-driver Ron Crellin posed for pictures. The results were posted, the pressmen spread the good news and that seemed to be that.

Then the trouble started. Just four minutes before the hour was up for protests a statement was posted by the organizers that Paddy had been penalized for arriving 14 minutes too early at a control in the early stages of the Rally and for servicing in the control area. This had the effect of dropping the Mini behind the two Cortinas. According to the statement this decision had been made by the Stewards acting on information supplied by the officials at the control in question.

Stuart Turner immediately lodged a counter protest but the Stewards refused to change their minds and the matter was passed forward to a National Board of Appeal. After an all-night sitting this too rejected it so Stuart then gave notice of intention to ask the RAC to raise the matter at the next meeting of the FIA. This upheld the Stewards' decision on evidence supplied by the officials and eventually the Fords were announced as victors.

The reason for Stuart's insistence in lodging the protest was that the action of the Stewards was not in accordance with international rallying regulations, that the control area in question was not satisfactorily defined owing to considerable congestion in the road, and it was believed that the control warning sign was obscured by parked vehicles. It was agreed by the control marshals at the time that no penalty was called for and the official road books were marked accordingly. Finally, quite a number of other competitors found themselves in the same position at this control but Paddy was the the only driver singled out for penalization.

Everyone left Greece with bitter feelings and, as far as BMC was concerned, even more determined to win – particularly over Ford. And that happened on the very next event.

Fall supreme

As a consolation for missing the Acropolis, Tony Fall acquired a car prepared by the Special Tuning Department for the Scottish Rally and won (his second win in two months) after a close battle with Vic Elford's Cortina and the Saab of Jerry Larsson.

Straight from Scotland Tony flew off to the Geneva Rally to compete in a Group I car and he was joined by Paddy Hopkirk who drove Group II. It was not a distinguished event for Paddy who retired with gearbox failure when in the lead, but Tony drove well to bring the Group I car into second place overall behind Gilbert Staepelaere's Cortina. Again the Minis won the Team Prize in company with the private cars of Georges Theiler and David Friswell.

Back to England for the London Rally, Tony proved that he was really on top form by leading all the way until three stages from the end when he was unlucky to roll on a treacherous stage in Gloucestershire which was subsequently closed because it was considered too dangerous.

Tony claimed his third international win of the season on the Polish Rally when he finished just ahead of Timo Makinen. Tony, driving a 970, was assisted by the handicap formula against the 1275 of Timo who was, I believe, also given the incorrect stage time on one occasion which dropped him down the leader board. This, however, did nothing to detract from the fine performances of the young Fall in this his first season with the team.

The Finnish War

By this time what was to become known as 'The Finnish War' between Timo Makinen and Rauno Aaltonen was beginning to brew quite splendidly. The two Finns were really very good friends but there was always a determined rivalry between them. Unquestionably Timo was always a little bit faster – in any car and in any circumstances – but the crafty Rauno knew that he could probably beat him if he saved his car just that little bit.

Timo was, I think, a little jealous of the publicity that Rauno received upon winning the Championship in 1965. While both the Finns were national heroes back home, there was no doubt that Rauno realized that his team mate probably had a bigger fan club, perhaps because the public always favoured the fun-loving Makinen rather than the studious Aaltonen. It was not unlike the attitude which many enthusiasts showed towards Mike Hawthorn and Stirling Moss.

Clearly such rivalry in the team was a very good thing, with each driver spurring his mate on to even faster performances. It did not really matter if either of them broke their cars, providing Paddy Hopkirk and Tony Fall were always waiting in the wings to take up the challenge – and this was usually the case. I certainly did nothing to discourage the 'war' during my term of office but the main jousters were the co-drivers Paul Easter and Henry Liddon. These two would never miss an opportunity of confusing their opposite number with a perfect piece of rallymanship. Paul would knock five seconds off Timo's time and tell Henry who would knock another five seconds off and then tell the little Finn that he would really have to get going on the next stage. The fact that Henry knocked an equal amount of Rauno's time and then Paul would knock something off again before reporting to Timo, probably had the desired effect of making both of them return increasingly faster times.

The 'war' also encouraged the Finns to think a lot about detailed improvements to their cars which was a very good thing. Timo would come over from Finland and bring with him some demon engine or suspension improvement that he had tried on his ice racing Minis back home. It would be handed over to Doug Watts with strict instructions that he was to have it on his car for the next event but that Rauno was not to be allowed to try it. Rauno would then come on the phone with some equally interesting experiment to be tried on his car for the forthcoming event. I would not have put it past Doug to try Timo's improvements on Rauno's car and experiment with Rauno's secret on Timo's!

Aaltonen 2–Makinen 2

The next four events on the 1966 programme took the two Finns to the Czech, 1000 Lakes, Alpine and the Three Cities Rallies – success being shared equally.

On the Czech Rally the lead alternated between Timo and Rauno as first one then the other set the fastest times. Timo lost some time with fuel starvation troubles, then Rauno had a slight accident on a stage which put Timo back in front. Finally it all rested on the round the houses race at Prague and, after a neck and neck battle, Timo had a rocker break on the last lap. Rauno was thus the victor but Timo was able to struggle across the line and make third place ahead of Bengt Soderstrom's Cortina. With the Group I car on loan to Sobislaw Zasada, the Polish Champion, the Team Prize went to the Minis.

Returning to his native Finland, Timo was able to turn the tables on Rauno on the 1000 Lakes Rally when he beat him to a close 1-2 victory, the pair leading Tom Trana (Volvo) and Bengt Soderstrom (Cortina) by a comfortable margin.

While Timo always found the 1000 Lakes to his liking, the long, fast Alpine Rally never suited his temperament. His performances in this French classic usually found him back on the sunny beach at Marseilles after the first day's motoring and the 1966 event was no exception. Timo stormed off into a dramatic lead only to drop out very early on with overheating and a blown head gasket. Paddy Hopkirk had an unlucky Alpine too and he was soon out with differential trouble. Tony Fall then fell by the wayside leaving Rauno Aaltonen with Henry Liddon to uphold Abingdon's honour and contest the lead with Gunther Klass (Porsche), Roger Clark (Cortina) and Jean Rolland (Alfa).

Then with a certain category win in sight, on the final run-in to Cannes, the Mini suffered a mysterious and complete electrical failure. By virtue of some hastily contrived wiring held in place by Henry they finished third overall but sadly lost their Coupe des Alpes award by some 20 seconds.

For the Munich–Vienna–Budapest Rally it was Timo's turn to take the honours and this win brought him to within only four points of the European Championship and to the all-important final round – the RAC Rally.

All star RAC

The line-up of works Minis for the 1966 RAC Rally, no fewer than seven cars, was the biggest ever entry for the Abingdon team, if not the most successful. In addition to the regular quartet of Makinen, Aaltonen, Hopkirk and Fall, cars were also provided for Harry Kallstrom, Simo Lampinen and Grand Prix star Graham Hill.

With the late Jim Clark joining the Ford team for this event, Stuart Turner was determined to have his share of the publicity so he signed Hill who was partnered by motoring correspondent Max Boyd. Despite a few driving lessons by Paddy at our favourite tank-testing course in Surrey, I think Graham would be the first to admit that he did not take to the Mini or to rallying and he was probably quite relieved when he retired with transmission troubles in the Lake District.

Simo Lampinen and Tony Ambrose also had quite a short rally when they rolled in Wales on the notorious Dovey stage. Simo is an immensely popular character, in the rallying world, whose talents and courage earn the highest respect from his fellow drivers and the mechanics. Born in Porvoo in Finland, where he worked in the family ski manufacturing business, Simo started rallying in 1961 after a remarkable recovery from polio in 1957. It was three years before he could even walk and his determination to be able to drive for as long and as fast as the best of his fellow countrymen is typical of his courage. Even today, although he has acquired the strength in his legs to drive as fast as anyone in events like the 10,000 mile London-to-Sydney Marathon which he so nearly won, he still has difficulty in walking more than a few hundred yards. It is a great pity that he only had two drives with the team.

Timo Makinen did not have a good R A C Rally either, for after an incredible run of fastest stage times that put him in the lead by a comfortable margin, what seemed like a winning run came to a sad end on the Yorkshire moors with a blown engine. It was, of course, also the end of Timo's bid for the Championship. Paddy Hopkirk, too, was unlucky – he was the leading British driver until he overshot a junction on a stage, reversed back and the transmission broke beyond repair.

It was Harry Kallstrom who proved that he was the man of the moment as far as the B M C team was concerned and, after a none too happy showing in previous British events with the works Minis, he justified his place in the team this time with a rousing second place overall behind Bengt Soderstrom's Cortina. Rauno Aaltonen could manage no better than fourth with Tony Fall finishing fifth – the Minis being 1-2-3 in class.

Turner bows out

The year 1966 had not brought the victories of the past season and it had not been a good year for international rallying. The opposition was beginning to get to grips with the Mini domination and clearly 1967 was to demand a tremendous effort by the team if they were to stay on top.

For Stuart Turner it was not a bad moment to decide to hang up his organization clip-board and take a temporary 'holiday' at Castrol, away from the hurly-burly of motor sport. It was not going to be easy to follow in his footsteps.

CHAPTER 9

HOPKIRK VICTORIOUS

It was just before Christmas 1966 that John Thornley called me to his oak-panelled office and sat me down in one of the big leather upright chairs by the bay window overlooking the MG works. John paced up and down in his usual manner in front of the stone fireplace beneath a classic oil painting of MGs at Brooklands. I knew that I had got the sack or promotion!

'Got a new job for you,' he said. 'Stuart Turner is leaving us and you're going to be the new Competitions Manager.'

That was the only time that I ever had a disagreement with John Thornley and, of course, I lost! I was allowed just one minute to stammer out as many excuses as I could think of why I could not do the job – then I was firmly told that it had already been decided that I was to lead the team. Stuart and I would do the Monte together and then I'd be on my own.

Certainly, I felt that my qualifications for doing the job were some-what slender. I had gone to Abingdon first as General Secretary of the Austin-Healey Club and, a year later, joined the staff of the BMC sports car magazine, *Safety Fast*. With my past interest in race time-keeping, Stuart had entrusted me to look after the organization of the MG entries in one or two events and I had been fortunate in having been to Sebring, Le Mans and the Targa Florio with the team, Stuart, at that time, was so busy winning rallies that he was probably quite pleased to have a keen youngster to take charge of the racing side which at that time didn't interest him.

Later I worked as Competitions Press Officer under Wilson Mc-Comb which had given me the opportunity to go on more events and, in particular, to find out something about the international rally scene. It was on these trips that I had got to know and respect the drivers and mechanics in the team, as well as those who served with the all-important trade support teams, Castrol and Dunlop in particular. No doubt I got the job on the strength of these associations rather than any technical know-how about competition cars or special knowledge

of the sport. Still, to be able to start off having a lot of friends made
the job much easier and I will always be grateful to them for the help
and guidance that they gave me.

Monte revenge

It was, therefore, with some trepidation that I moved over the road
into the hallowed Competitions Department and squeezed in along-
side Stuart Turner in his diminutive office. Preparations were in full
swing for the 1967 Monte and it was an awesome experience to be
thrown in at the deep end and try to catch up with the organization
of the most complex event of all. I shudder to think now of the
responsibilities that were thrust upon me for that event, perhaps the
hardest fought Monte of all and the one that the BMC team so
desperately wanted to win to avenge the disqualification of 1966.
Many people thought that we would not have entered again after the
treatment we received in the previous year but that would have
seemed like surrender. I am sure that it was right to go back, win or
lose, and put up the hardest fight to prove the point.

Perhaps the Monte organizers' new tyre restrictions for 1967 were
aimed at a handicap against the Minis, but certainly they were aimed
to reduce the mounting costs of competing in this event and to narrow
the gap between the private owner and the works team. Unfortunately
the regulations had exactly the opposite effect.

Most teams took more tyres that year to Monte than on previous
events and, although only eight could be chosen for the Common
Run and the Mountain Circuit, works teams had an enormous selection
available. As for the private owner he had to make do with the best
collection of tyres he could carry and afford and, with the restrictions
for the works crews, there was no chance of service along the route
and therefore no opportunities to pick up spares on the way if he
found himself running short of rubber. To ask a man to drive quickly
on ice and snow with worn tyres is as dangerous as suggesting that he
does so on worn brake pads.

There were few dramas for the very strong five-car Mini team
on the run-in sections, all of the works cars of Hopkirk, Makinen,
Aaltonen, Fall and Lampinen arriving in good shape. Only Paddy,
who started from Athens, had met bad weather and he had had to do
some shovelling through Yugoslavia.

Careful selection of the eight tyres, aided by the work of the ice note crews surveying the stages out in the mountains, found the Minis well placed after the Monaco–Chambéry–Monaco leg. Paddy was lying second to Vic Elford's Porsche 911S with Timo and Rauno not far behind, ahead of the Lancias of Ove Andersson and Leo Cella.

With conditions remaining critical with patchy ice and a lot of dry roads, the Minis opted for almost dry-weather tyres for the Mountain Circuit, Rauno gaining a benefit over his team mates by going for plain and only partly studded Weathermasters. This selection, with a well-judged drive and sparing use of his studs, expertly guided by Henry Liddon, paid off and Rauno returned a classic performance to win by only 12 seconds from Ove Andersson's Lancia after several recounts of the times, which was as heart-stopping as the 1966 scrutineering sessions! Paddy did not seem to be able to maintain his previous supremacy and he could finish no higher than sixth. Timo dropped way down the field when he hit a great boulder that mysteriously fell into the middle of the road just as he was passing, smashing the starter motor, distributor and oil cooler.

The timing of that rock fall was the subject of much lighthearted suspicion by the British contingent and, during the celebrations for Rauno on the plane coming home, the Abingdon mechanics, led by Brian Moylan, composed this little ditty to be sung to the tune of 'Clementine'.

> On the Monte in the mountains
> Racing onwards through the night,
> Was a little Mini-Cooper
> With its lights all shining bright.
>
> Red it was and oh so eager
> And its crew was eager too,
> Faster, faster and still faster
> Showing all what they could do.
>
> Timo driving, Paul beside him
> Reading pace notes as a guide,
> Then disaster came and struck them
> Hurtling down the mountainside.
>
> No-one knows who shoved the rock down,
> But Timo said he thought
> Must have been the 'little people'
> Giving Paddy their support!

That Monte win was the sweetest revenge and the perfect leaving present for Stuart Turner who had now provided a Monte victory for each of his three drivers.

Another luckless Swedish

After the Monte, the two Finns were dispatched to contest the Swedish Rally but, as usual, this was not to be our lucky event. Timo Makinen was forced to drop out on only the second special stage with brake trouble while Rauno Aaltonen lost time after a spectacular accident. While progressing well up the leader board in pursuit of Simo Lampinen's Saab and the eventual winner, Bengt Soderstrom's Cortina, Rauno collided with a snow bank on a stage and the Mini rolled end over end, finally finishing up back on its wheels and driveable. During the incident, however, the rear window had fallen out, scattering the contents of the car along the stage for hundreds of yards. Rauno and co-driver Henry Liddon lost some time collecting their belongings and stuffing them back into the battered Mini, but gamely struggled on to finish third overall, despite the cold and the effects of exhaust fumes which came in through the windowless car. This was, at least, the first time that an Abingdon Mini had ever finished the Swedish!

Pushing our luck!

The tiny village of Badalucco sits perched high in the mountains behind San Remo. The road down from the village to the coast takes a tortuous route through the vineyards. You could describe the narrow road as 'downhill all the way' – some might even believe that it would be possible to free-wheel the 20 km from the village into the town below. Amongst them, apparently, were the organizers and competitors in the 1967 Italian Rally of the Flowers. The story of how Paddy Hopkirk gained his second place can now be told!

It was at Badalucco that the final special stage of the Rally finished and, less than a mile from the end, Paddy's Mini – holding a slender lead from the Renault-Gordini of Jean Piot, broke a drive shaft coupling. Fortunately, he was able to summon help from a tractor and, with a push over the final brow, he coasted down to the service point where Doug Watts and I were waiting. Paddy had lost his lead but he would be sure of second place if he could reach the final control in

San Remo. Although we had a spare drive shaft on board the service car, that final road section was very tight and there was not time to change it.

'Push us down the hill with the service car,' suggested Paddy. 'Hang back if there are any photographers around. I'll keep the engine going and pretend to be driving it normally.'

Doug and I leapt into the car, one of our faithful 4-litre Princess 'R's, and began the long push. Fortunately, the bumpers were near enough the same height and we did not do too much damage, despite the fact that the co-driver Ron Crellin was worried about the time and continually encouraged us to go faster.

Doug drove the big heavy car like a demon, down through the hairpins, although Paddy had a more alarming ride with no power to control the free-wheeling car. On many steep stretches he was able to run away from the lumbering Princess 'R' and then, around a corner, we would meet up again with a resounding crash which would propel the little Mini onwards!

There was a time control in a village half-way down the hill, for-tunately on a steep incline so we were able to give the Mini a big push, back off and let Paddy 'drive' into the control while we motored sedately by and waited for him around the next corner. Feigning violent clutch slip, Paddy slowly gathered speed out of the control and soon we were on our way again, without anyone aware that the Mini was not struggling home under its own power.

As we approached San Remo, more and more photographers were out to get a picture of what they thought was the winning Mini. Always Doug was able to back off just in time, leaving Paddy and Ron to give them a cheery smile and a wave while blipping the engine merrily to simulate the gear changes.

Our main fear, however, was the traffic on the San Remo coast road but Doug did a magnificent job nudging the Mini through the jams. Not even the traffic policeman waving the Rally cars through really appreciated what was going on.

The final drama came a few hundred yards from the control which was situated in a big car park at the exit to a long tunnel. Doug got up to around 60 mph in the tunnel and backed off just in time to eject a terrified Paddy into the daylight! With lights ablaze and horn blaring Paddy performed a neat handbrake turn around a bewildered police-man on a traffic island and had just enough speed to free-wheel into the control area. This final episode was watched by many hundreds of spectators, local T V film crews and the entire organizing committee who welcomed Paddy as the worthy runner-up.

Although we fully expected that our little game would have been detected, and we would have had to admit it if we had been challenged, nobody murmured a word and Paddy and Ron got their second place. The only man who I felt was just a little puzzled as to how Paddy had either had time to replace the drive shaft or had managed to free-wheel all that way was John Davenport, the co-driver of the third placed Lancia driven by Ove Andersson!

A Safari Mini

As part of their Monte-winning prize, Rauno Aaltonen and Henry Liddon took a Mini on the East African Safari over Easter. The car bristled with Aaltonen-type gadgets for Safari motoring – hand-operated screen wipers, handles for lifting the car out of the mud, foot-plates for bouncing it along muddy roads, exhaust extensions for fording rivers and a hydrolastic pump built into the system and mounted on the rear seat so that the ride height could be quickly adjusted.

A Mini was never rated as a suitable Safari car, let alone a wet Safari, and 1967 was unfortunately one of the wettest. The car finally expired when mud and water got into the engine through the inadequate carburetter air filters.

Racing at Sebring

Straight from his fifth win on the Circuit of Ireland, albeit this time against little opposition, Paddy Hopkirk flew off to Sebring to drive a Mini in the Four Hour Saloon Car Race with John Rhodes.

On our previous trips to Sebring with the M G and Austin-Healey teams, we had been interested and frustrated spectators in the 'sedan' race which preceded the 12 hour sports car classic. The standard of competition, particularly in the 1300 cc class, was pretty pathetic and B M C in America suggested that it would be fun to demonstrate the Mini in the hands of Hopkirk and Rhodes. For the 1967 race, therefore, we entered one of our old Group II rally cars which proved highly competitive and gave the crowd a fine opportunity of seeing how a Mini should really be handled on a race track.

The start, with some 70 cars on the grid, was an absolute shambles, the people at the back could not even see the starter's flag! As the cars were lined up according to engine size, the Mini was right at the back but Paddy, who took the first spell, did a magnificent get-away and was already half-way through the field before he passed the starting line!

The car ran faultlessly and maintained a good overall placing while leading the 1300 cc class. Then, after two hours, Paddy came in to refuel and hand over to John. The brisk pit stop went as planned and Rhodes soon took the Mini back into the race. Everything was running according to plan, then the Mini came in for an unscheduled stop after only a further one hour's running, John complaining of fuel starvation. The car was quickly refuelled again when it was discovered that the gravity fuel tank in the pits was pumping in both air and fuel. Having calculated the amount of fuel put in according to the length of time the nozzle was open, obviously the tank was running dry. This second stop had now dropped the Mini to second place in the class behind a works Lancia. But as four o'clock, the end of the race, approached the Mini was back in the lead by half a lap.

The finishing arrangements at Sebring are unique in that the timing line is situated on the corner before the pits yet the finishing line, where the chequered flag is displayed, is half-way along the pit straight. Rhodes crossed the timing line just before the four o'clock deadline with the Mini completely out of fuel again and spluttering to a halt on the pit road, not having taken the chequered flag on the circuit. There were large groans from the BMC supporters as the Lancia swept past the flag but all was not lost. More fuel was poured into the Mini and John set off to complete his last lap, fighting his way through the crowded pit road. He finally crossed the line four minutes inside the time allowed to complete the last lap.

When it was announced that the Mini had been beaten by the Lancia I took my lap charts and time sheets to the timekeepers and we were able to prove that, in fact, the Mini qualified according to the race rules as the class winner. Not surprisingly, the Lancia team were furious – it was just like old rallying times again!

Porsche chasing on the Tulip

Hot favourites for the Tulip Rally that year were Porsche, as the results were to be decided by scratch times and the going was dry and most of the tests were uphill which was more suited to rear-engined rear-wheel-drive cars.

Vic Elford's 911S managed to beat Timo Makinen by only 46 seconds, however, and Rauno Aaltonen, in the second works Mini, was right behind. Timo's performance was the more remarkable because a piston broke up half-way through the event and the car would not run for long without frequent topping-up of oil and plug changes. Julian Vernaeve, who always goes well on the Tulip, helped us to win the Manufacturers Team Prize in his own car navigated by Mike Wood.

Paddy's Acropolis

Of the wins that the team scored during my 'reign' I have always felt that the 1967 Acropolis was the most rewarding. The Minis, having campaigned in Greece for four years and dropped out every time when in the lead (or, as in 1966, been disqualified from first place) it was fitting that Paddy Hopkirk, the moral victor in 1966, should come through to final victory. But this was no easy win.

From the start, the Abingdon trio of Makinen, Aaltonen and Hopkirk set the pace against the main opposition, Ove Andersson (Lancia) and Bengt Soderstrom (Cortina). Then Rauno was involved in a terrifying accident with a non-competing Volkswagen which was going the wrong way on a stage that was supposed to be closed. Rauno was hospitalized with mild concussion and co-driver Henry Liddon suffered some big bumps and bruises, but they both recovered in time to join in the victory celebrations. This left Timo Makinen to take up the challenge but soon he was out after troubles with a broken rear sub frame and a grumbling gearbox.

So it was Paddy alone who soldiered on to the finish, with a beautifully judged drive aided by skillful guidance from co-driver Ron Crellin. Only a comic driving test, the Parnis hill climb and the Tatoi race could now prevent the Mini from winning. On the driving test Paddy proved that he had forgotten nothing of his old pylon-bashing skills and on the hill climb he made quite sure of victory by beating his nearest rivals, Andersson and Soderstrom, by some three seconds, despite being baulked by a car that had set off four minutes ahead of him!

The final circuit race, which did not affect the results provided you finished, was a great spectacle as the three leading cars diced together. But on the fourth lap the Mini gave up the ghost with no bearings, Paddy wisely stopped just short of the finishing line and, at

Preparations in the Competitions Department at Abingdon for the 1966 Monte
Carlo Rally

Interior of a works Mini for the 1968 Monte Carlo Rally

All the Monte winners! *Above*, Paddy Hopkirk and Henry Liddon with the 1071 Mini-Cooper 'S' at the 1964 Racing Car Show. *Below*, Timo Makinen and Paul Easter with the Group 2 1275 on the 1965 Monte

The team look far from sad having been robbed of their 1-2-3 Monte victory in 1966. *Left to right, on the roof*: Paul Easter, Henry Liddon, Tony Ambrose. *On the bonnet*: Rauno Aaltonen, Timo Makinen and Paddy Hopkirk

Below, 1967 Monte winners, Rauno Aaltonen and Henry Liddon return to Gatwick on the BMC charter plane

Three more 1966 winners, Timo Makinen/Paul Easter. Munich-Vienna-Budapest Rally

Rauno Aaltonen/Henry Liddon, Czech Rally

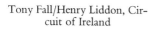

Tony Fall/Henry Liddon, Circuit of Ireland

New partnership, Ron Crellin joins Paddy Hopkirk for the 1966 R A C Rally –
the team that was to enjoy such success in 1967

Harry Kallstrom, runner-up on the 1966 R A C Rally, demonstrates the perfect
cornering attitude achieved with left-foot braking

Marcus Chambers
1954–1962

Stuart Turner
1962–1967

Peter Browning
1967–1970

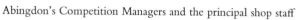

Abingdon's Competition Managers and the principal shop staff

Doug Watts
Shop Supervisor

Tommy Wellman
Foreman

Den Green
Deputy Foreman

Bill Price
Deputy Competition Manager

Winners on the rough or on tarmac. *Above*, Paddy Hopkirk and Ron Crellin scrabble for grip on their way to winning the 1966 Austrian Alpine Rally. *Below*, Rauno Aaltonen and Henry Liddon racing at Zandvoort to win the touring category on the 1967 Tulip Rally

Timo Makinen's 1000 Lakes Rally hat-trick in 1965 *(above)*, 1966 *(right)* and 1967 *(below)* despite doing most of one stage with the bonnet up!

The man responsible for most of the development and testing of the works
Minis – Abingdon's Chief Technician, Cliff Humphries

The Mini with the mostest, the car built for Rauno Aaltonen and Henry Liddon
for the 1967 East African Safari

Action stations at a service point for Rauno Aaltonen on the 1967 Monte Carlo Rally. Bill Price, between Rauno and bespectacled Henry Liddon, directs operations. Chief Storeman Neville Challis goes in search of parts behind the car. Mick Hogan in the foreground prepares for a wheel change

Nail biting was much in fashion during 1966/7 with constant fears of protests and disqualifications. Paddy Hopkirk, mechanic Dudley Pike and Tony Fall don't seem too concerned if anyone should find out about the little 'pushing' episode on the 1967 Flowers Rally told in Chapter 9

Pulling away from a service point on the 1967 Tulip Rally, Timo Makinen and
Paul Easter motor on to a win in the touring category

The author with Clive Baker testing the Group 6 970 Minis at Castle Combe
before the 84 Hours Marathon at the Nurburgring

Last appearance of the works Minis on the Monte Carlo Rally was in 1968 when the team finished third, fourth and fifth, beaten by Porsche. *Above,* Tony Fall and Mike Wood who were placed fourth

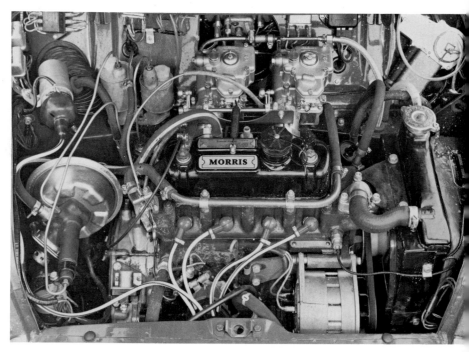

The Group 2 engine for the 1968 Monte Carlo Rally showing the controversial split Weber carburettors

For the 1968 Monte Carlo Rally, the works Minis had available a total of 731 tyres and 12 optional patterns and stud formations. From top to bottom of the pile, CR70 racing tyre, Green Spot R7L10 racing tyre, plain SP44 dry compound, plain SP44 wet compound, SP44 half-studded graded stud protrusion dry compound, SP44 half-studded graded stud protrusion wet compound, SP44 three-quarter stud graded stud protrusion, SP44 with full graded stud protrusion, SP44 fully studded, fully studded snow pattern, 'knobbly' snow tyre, 'chisel' snow tyre

Tyres by Dunlop

Mini racer John Handley applied himself very effectively to the Tour de France in 1969 and, with Paul Easter, was all set for a class win and a place in the top ten when he crashed on the last hill climb

John Handley leads John Rhodes with two of the Abingdon racers at Crystal Palace, 1969

The fuel injection rally car that never ran, entered for the cancelled 1967 RAC Rally, and only run on the one televised special stage; driver Timo Makinen, startled passenger Tony Fall! *Below*, the fuel injection engine

Televised rallycross proved to be a very effective way of breaking up old rally cars, especially when John Rhodes and Paddy Hopkirk appeared in the same race! The gentleman in the background going the conventional way around the corner is Graham Hill

Last success for the works Minis was on the 1970 Scottish Rally when Paddy Hopkirk with Tony Nash won their class and finished runner-up in their Group 6 Mini Clubman 1275

the end of the 30 minute race, restarted to cross the line a very popular winner.

Ytterbring and Persson

It would be a foolish competition manager who was not always on the look-out for up and coming driving talent and who did not give them the opportunity of a works drive if the budget and programme allowed. One of the young Swedes who impressed me, both as a driver and as the sort of man who would slot well into the team, was Lars Ingvar Ytterbring and his equally pleasant co-driver Lars Persson.

This pair drove for us on several occasions, their first performance being on the Scottish Rally in 1967 when they finished a very creditable second overall – a performance that they repeated on the same event the following year. They formed a good relationship with the boys in the Special Tuning Department who prepared several cars for them to rally both in Europe and at home in Sweden.

They were a highly professional partnership, very polite in true Scandinavian fashion and always tremendously grateful for any help that they received. Like the Morley twins, they went rallying in immaculate smartly pressed suits or sports wear. They never seemed to get dirty on an event and Ytterbring's car was usually returned to Abingdon without a scratch on it. He learnt to handle right-hand-drive cars very quickly and, after some excellent performances on forestry rallies, was starting to go well on tarmac too. I was very sorry that our later programme did not allow us to develop the full potential of this pair.

Geneva confusion

The 1967 Geneva Rally finished in some confusion. The Geneva Rally itself counted only for cars in Groups I and III, so the entries in Groups II, IV, V and VI were put into a separate classification and 'entered' in another rally – the Criterium de Crans-sur-Sierre. When it was all over two completely different sets of results were announced which put Vic Elford's 911S first in the Geneva Rally with the Minis of Tony Fall / Mike Wood and Julian Vernaeve / Henry Liddon first and second overall in the Criterium event. The confused results did no justice to the very fine performance of the Mini crews against the more fancied Porsche opposition.

Although this was Julian Vernaeve's first drive in an Abingdon-prepared Mini, he was no stranger in the team having helped us win several team prizes in the past. Julian, who comes from Gent in Belgium seems equally at home rallying or racing. He won the Belgian Rally Championship in 1962 and 1963 and their Saloon Car Championship in 1964, driving his own cars, mostly with engines prepared by Don Moore. When he drove for the B M C team he never failed to achieve what was demanded from him – indeed he often provided sensational results. He is a driver who always seems to go best on tarmac events which he can practise – his Tulip successes being particularly notable. Julian was famous at Abingdon for his regular appearances with a scruffy Mini van into which he would pack as many scrap and second-hand parts as he could scrounge to keep his own Minis competitive! In return he never failed to reciprocate this assistance with generous hospitality whenever the team passed through Belgium.

Danube disqualification

Any rally, particularly if it ventures through faraway countries, can be won or lost on 'documentation'. A team manager's nightmare is to have a potential rally winner fail to win because someone has not got the right piece of paper in the right place at the right time. And that's what happened to Rauno Aaltonen on the 1967 Danube Rally.

At the start in Prague there was considerable disagreement between Rauno and the officials as to what visa was necessary for the Finn to enter Hungary. It was finally agreed that he did not need one but, if this was wrong information, he could easily obtain one at the frontier. When Rauno reached the border, he found that he did need a visa but that the officials refused to give him one on the spot. The Mini was therefore out of the Rally.

My disappointment was only redeemed by the fact that the Austin 1800 driven by Tony Fall and Mike Wood won the Rally on this its first international outing.

1000 Lakes hat-trick

After a tremendous battle with the Saab of Simo Lampinen, Timo Makinen just won the 1000 Lakes Rally for the third year running. But the event produced a spectacular drama when the bonnet flew open on a stage. The car had been overheating so Timo had removed the spot lamps and was running with the bonnet slightly open, held closed only by the rubber safety straps. But on one enormous 'yump' the bonnet flew up and Timo had to drive on for some 10 km peering out of an open door. Even so he only dropped 19 seconds on the fastest man!

Minis on the Marathon

In 1966, the second year when the old Spa-Sofia-Liege Rally became the 84 Hours Marathon de la Route at the Nurburgring, we surprised everyone – including ourselves – by winning outright with an M G B driven by Andrew Hedges and Julian Vernaeve. When the rather complicated regulations appeared for the 1967 event it seemed that a 1 litre car would stand a very good chance of beating the formula. We therefore entered a pair of Group 6 970 cc cars, the driving teams being Andrew Hedges / Julian Vernaeve / Tony Fall and Clive Baker / Roger Enever / Alec Poole. The cars had lightweight bodies but the only mechanical novelties were the auxiliary forward-facing water radiators and an electric pump which enabled the drivers to top up the oil in the sump on the move from an auxiliary tank in the cockpit.

Both cars ran completely according to plan and, with the help of a lot of wet weather and fog, the Minis climbed up the leader board on scratch as well as on the reliability classification. Just after half distance Clive Baker had a throttle cable break, out on the circuit, and the repair cost a 26 minute penalty and put this car right out of the running. I therefore instructed Alec Poole, who took over, to forget our carefully planned schedule and rev limits and go flat out to try and catch up with the leaders. Alec made excellent progress until he misjudged one of the Nurburgring's deceptive bends in the fog, the car went off the road and ended up on its roof, out of the event. Alec was completely unhurt but very annoyed!

By now the Hedges / Vernaeve / Fall car was up amongst the leading Porsches on scratch and the surviving Mini actually took the lead with only 10 hours to run. But then one of the wheel bearings had to be changed, the hub refused to budge and the pit stop took longer than planned. Vic Elford took the Porsche back into the lead but the gallant little 970 finished second overall and won the special reliability award based on penalties gained for the minimum time spent in the pits. Apart from the problem with the wheel bearing, the Mini covered 5,500 trouble-free racing miles in the 84 hours.

Hopkirk's Alpine

In the long rallying career Paddy Hopkirk has often benefited by practising the old motto 'that to win you must first finish'. This is more difficult to achieve in rallying than any other branch of the sport and there has been no finer demonstration than Paddy's victory in the 1967 Alpine Rally.

The Minis were hardly competitive entries from the start and the crews knew that they would be completely outclassed by the opposition and could only win on reliability. Thus, from the traditional starting point in Marseilles, it was the Porsche of Vic Elford that made the running along with the Renault-Alpines of Gerard Larrousse and Jean Vinatier.

The first B M C casualty was Tony Fall who went off the road at Sigale and hit a wall. Not far up the road Rauno Aaltonen stopped with gearbox failure. Timo Makinen seemed to be having a longer Alpine than usual but, by the end of the first stage, at the Alpe d' Huez ski resort, he was in trouble with an overheating engine, although lying third overall behind the leading Renault-Alpines. Paddy's car was in perfect shape and lying in a comfortable seventh place.

On to the second leg, Timo moved up to second place with the retirement of Jean Vinatier only to drop out with a succession of brake troubles and, finally, an overheating engine. With a carefully judged performance and, in particular, superb pace note work by Ron Crellin in the fog, Paddy slowly overhauled the leaders – actually overtaking Gerard Larrousse on one foggy stage. With the later retirement of the leading Alpine, Paddy gained his lead, and after a classic drive, was able to return to Marseilles with a three minute margin over the G T A Alfa-Romeos of Bernard Consten and Jean Claude Gamet, all that remained of the serious opposition.

Those Corsican fanbelts

To return home from an incredibly expensive sortie like the Tour de Corse and have to tell the 'powers that be' that your two cars retired on the very first stage with a fault as elementary as slipping fanbelts is not a very happy thought! But that's what happened on the 1967 event, the two Minis of Paddy Hopkirk and Rauno Aaltonen lasting only a few kilometres over the very first stage when slipping fanbelts caused immediate and irreparable overheating troubles.

This was despite the belts being checked and adjusted before the start.

It was little consolation to discover afterwards that the manufacturers had supplied a batch of faulty belts. It was just our luck that storeman Neville Challis had to pick those two belts from the bin at Abingdon. Despite this disastrous outing to Corsica, and the disappointing last-minute cancellation of the R A C Rally because of foot and mouth disease, 1967 had been a profitable year. Against all form the works Minis were still winning, having claimed victory in three great classics in one season – the Monte, Acropolis and Alpine.

CHAPTER 10

MINI TYRES

Tyre design over the past five years has played a vital role in the aim for the ultimate performance with all cars and in all branches of motor sport. The Mini has been no exception and, in both rallying and racing, the works cars could not have achieved their success without the co-operation of the Dunlop Company who provided tyres for the Abingdon team since it was formed in 1954. Such is the significance of Dunlop's association with Abingdon, and with the Mini in particular, that many projects involving new equipment were given the same priority as their Formula 1 activities.

The story of the evolution of competition tyres for the Mini is complex, but it has such a bearing on the success of the works team cars, that I feel it is worthy of a chapter of its own. It is one aspect of the sport which very few people appreciate and it is typical of the behind-the-scenes effort that the trade companies make to support the manufacturers.

For their co-operation in writing this chapter I am very grateful to Dunlop's former chief racing tyre designer, Iain Mills and to their rally manager, Jeremy Ferguson. Iain has never failed, at a time when he has been desperately involved with Formula 1 affairs, to help us with fresh thoughts on Mini tyre problems. Abingdon will always owe a big debt to Jeremy Ferguson, and to his predecesors, David Hiam and Oliver Speight, for the enthusiastic way in which they have always made sure that the team has had the right tyres at the right time and in the right place.

It was *Motor's* famous cartoonist, Russell Brockbank, who very early on illustrated the basic handicap of the Mini. He portrayed a Mini rocketing past a Jaguar on the motorway, the Jaguar driver remarking to his passenger, 'If the good Lord had meant cars that size to do 100 mph he'd have given them larger wheels.' Indeed, it has been the fitting of larger wheels or, more to the point, larger tyres that would get more rubber on to the road, that has so often been the 'achilles heel' of the Mini in competitions.

Basically, a tyre provides four main functions. It carries the weight of the car, it drives the car (and stops it, which is much the same job), it assists with the steering and it assists with the cornering. With front-wheel-drive the front tyres are asked to perform all four functions; with rear-wheel-drive the work load is shared rather more fairly. With the Mini there is the additional problem – around 65% of the total weight is upon the front wheels.

Under normal road driving conditions, front-wheel-drive must be considered better than rear-wheel-drive. In the event of understeer in cornering too fast, or a front-wheel skid, the natural reaction for the general motorist is to take his foot off the accelerator pedal. This, with the front-wheel-drive, has the desired effect of reducing the slip or skid, providing better grip for the front tyres which tucks the nose of the car in towards the apex of the corner and probably away from danger. Only the experienced driver used to rear-wheel-drive and of putting his foot down to bring the rear of the car round when in the same circumstances, may find this front-wheel-drive technique a little strange at first. But then being an experienced driver it would not take him very long to adapt his technique.

Rally tyres

For the first three years of rallying, the works Minis presented no tyre problems. The 850s ran on normal Durabands on 3½ in. steel wheels, and for the snow and ice on the Monte Carlo Rally, the popular bolt-through tungsten carbide studs were used. The 997 Mini-Coopers also ran on standard Durabands and, later on, Weathermasters, without any dramas.

When Rauno Aaltonen and Timo Makinen joined the team in 1963, there began more serious thinking about rally tyres, and particularly studded tyres for the Monte. The Finns introduced all sorts of strange things from their home country, including vicious 'chisels' and 'spikes' which were remoulded on to standard covers. At this time too came the idea to have SP3s and the cross-ply CW44 fitted with push-in studs.

The 1964 Alpine Rally saw the first use on the Minis of racing tyres for rallies, the 5·00 L-10 R6 proving exceptionally good in wet or dry conditions on road tarmac. Later the R6 and R7 were used with equal success on the smoother dirt roads where the drivers found advantages in cornering as the sharp shoulder of the racing tyres 'knifed' into the loose to give better cornering grip than the conventional rounded shoulder of the road tyre. The R6, and later the R7, stood up remarkably well on rough roads and its racing pattern gave adequate traction in all but the most muddy conditions.

By the Monte of 1965 the tyre options for the Mini were growing steadily and the Abingdon team of that year used R6 racers, SP3, the new SP44 and various Scandinavian 'spikes' and 'chisels'. A special version of the SP44 was introduced for the following Monte. This had an extra block on the centre to the tread to increase the stud platform and to allow an increase in the studding of up to 400/500 studs.

Inevitably when talking about rally tyres for the Minis one talks only of the Monte because this was the event on which major developments on rally tyres appeared. On all the other events the works Minis used the latest racing tyres that were available or the SP44.

The works Minis were not alone in having sophisticated tyre developments for the Monte. Although the organizers move, to restrict the number of tyres used for the final tests of the 1967 event to eight only, was aimed at reducing costs to all competitors, many feel that the new rules were set to handicap the Minis. In practice the restrictions proved no such handicap and they did little to cut down the costs to the works teams for it was still the number of types of tyres that were available for the crews to choose from that mattered. Thus the BMC/Dunlop plan for the 1967 event included no fewer than 572 tyres for the five works Minis.

But in the following year there were 731 tyres available for the four works Minis! The list of quantities and the various tyres available on this occasion were as follows:

36	145 – 10 SP3 with modified pattern, half studded
140	dry compound SP44 with graded stud protrusion
72	wet compound SP44 with graded stud protrusion
72	dry compound SP44 three-quarter studded
72	dry compound SP44 with full studs graded protrusion
72	dry compound SP44 with full studs
40	chisels
40	knobs
35	SP 564 'Hakka' pattern snow tyres fully studded
24	dry and wet compound plain SP44
64	Green spot 5·00 L-10 racers
64	CR70 5.00 L-10 green spot racers

The novelties of this year included the use of wet and dry compounds for all of the SP44s which also had an extra rubber depth to stabilize the bottom flange of the studs. The selection of the wet or dry compound was not only determined by the 'sticky' qualities of the tyre tread on the road, but it also affected the wear rate of the stud and its holding capacity in the tyre when running upon partly dry roads. This was also the first appearance of the new Dunlop snow tyre, an improved version of the Scandinavian Hakkapelita.

Finally, 1968 was the year of graded stud protrusion. This idea was another innovation introduced by the Finns, and although Dunlop stud technicians agreed with the theory, they were doubtful whether in practice there were advantages. Certainly it caused the biggest confusion and complication of the Monte tyre plan!

The idea was that the stud protrusion was graded across the tyre, the shallowest protrusion being upon the outside of the tyre with the longest protrusion on the inside. This improved the handling of the car in the corners on ice or snow. The straight driving grip was provided by the protrusion on the inside shoulder while, in cornering, the pressure on the outside shoulder forced the studs through the rubber. It also meant that the shallower studs lasted longer when running upon dry roads. The studs were also placed into the tread blocks in a special pattern, one into the leading block and two into the trailing block. This helped to reduce the wear and the tendency for the studs to come out when running upon dry roads.

The grading of the studs and their position in the tread blocks meant that the tyres were now 'handed' and it was essential that they were put on the correct side of the car. We therefore devised a colour marking code, blue and red to denote wet and dry compounds and green and yellow for the off-side and near-side of the car.

Racing tyres

Iain Mills talks of the philosophy of racing car tyre design as generations, there having been five such generations to date as far as the Mini is concerned. Within each generation there are many minor improvements effected by change of tread pattern, casing, compound or tread width. The generations really show the break in the then-current thoughts of racing tyre design. The first two generations were directed by the late Vic Barlow and Terry Hampton and then by Jack Leonard. From the third generation onwards Iain Mills was in charge of the projects.

The only requirement of the first Mini racing tyre was that it should offer rather better handling characteristics than the road tyre. Dunlop therefore took their road pattern mould, the D2/103, and put a nylon low-angle casing on it with the racing D7 tread compound. In dimensions this first racing tyre was the same as the old road tyre. It did the job well by simply changing the handling of the Mini from the characteristic insensitive steering and understeering handling to that of fairly instant response, considerably harsher but more balanced handling.

This first generation tyre worked well until the Mini began to develop power in the range of 80-85 bhp when it became clear that more rubber was wanted on the road. Thus in January 1964 the first Mini racing tyre proper came on the scene. These early Mini tyres paralleled early developments in the Formula I field – the adoption of slightly wider tyres with a lower aspect ratio, bigger tread width, more square shape on wider rims and with lower pressures.

The first of four developments in the second generation tyre was the well-known R6 (CR48) pattern with the green spot compound. This proved pretty adequate until midway through the 1965 season when Mini engines gained a further 10 bhp. Dunlop met this by introducing their Mark I CR 65 pattern, the same that was coming into use for Formula I. It was expected that the CR48 would be used for dry conditions only, with CR65 being used only in the wet. But then both Mini and Formula I drivers presented problems when they found that the CR65 gave considerable advantages in the dry as well as in the wet. Very quickly a Mark II pattern had to be evolved by reducing the number of ribs across the tyre which, with the Mini, meant a reduction of one complete rib. It was at this stage that the white spot compound was introduced, the first of the all-synthetic more sophisticated compounds that were soon to become the fashion.

This led to more problems with pattern stability and these were the days when John Rhodes in the Cooper Car Company Mini could achieve little more than seven or eight laps on a set of tyres when driving at 'ten tenths' in the style for which he was famed. A change of pattern to CR70 solved that problem for about one year and this, and the CR65 Mark II, proved to be very good when used in green (dry) and white (wet) spot compounds.

The Minis handling problems by now demanded that one should adopt different tyre equipment at the front and rear. To achieve the required balance CR65 was used at the rear with CR70 at the front.

Although there was little difference in tread widths, the combination of patterns gave the front end the desired higher stability than the rear.

With the Cooper cars producing yet more power for the 1966 season there were further troubles. There was still a lack of adhesion because the tyre was too small, and now the tyre was overheating and losing its stability. This was particularly marked when racing upon an oily track, and this was usually the case when the saloon car race was the last event of the day. Quite often the Minis were able to record competitive times in practice when the track was in good condition, only to find themselves running some 10 secs per lap slower in the race. Furthermore the lap times in the race inevitably got slower and slower as tyre temperatures went up into the 95-100 degs centigrade mark, when the whole tyre pattern and the compound lost its stability.

Much the same problem was now facing the Formula I drivers so it seemed logical to apply the Formula I development to the Mini. It was at this stage too that the Mini racing tyre project was to receive equal priorities with Formula I requirements. It was decided to make a miniature Formula I tyre and make it almost square like a box with a different casing construction so that it would remain square. This got around the major problem of accommodating a wider tread width within the limited space available under the Mini wheel arches.

To achieve this, Dunlop faced a number of problems. They did not know very much about wide tyres in Formula I in those days, and they had to go to a very different casing construction from that of the early tyre. There was fresh thinking, therefore, with aspects such as profile shapes, general tread behaviour at speeds and sidewall stability.

In the remarkably quick time of less than two months, Dunlop produced the new CR81 plain mould design onto which a handcut pattern was made. This early tyre was not assymetric, it had very sharp shoulders and it initially proved to be fractionally faster than rival tyres. But still there were problems.

The tyre was still losing stability and grip when it got hot so the first thing to be done was to go to a new compound that wore the same, that gripped much better, that gave the same stability at high temperatures, was soft and sticky enough at all temperatures, yet would tolerate very high temperatures without damage. Dick Squires, Dunlop's demon compound expert, produced the necessary goods by evolving a system of mixing together three basically different compounds to make a unique bond. This was known as 236 compound and it is still in use today as Dunlop's basic dry weather compound.

The CR81 in handcut form with this compound was introduced in May 1967 for use by the Cooper cars only. But it was not long before these cars were producing some 100–105 bhp and now the inside shoulder of the tyre was getting extremely hot. This was partly because to get the right handling characteristics a lot of negative camber was being used. Down the straight, when the car was accelerating, the inside of the tyre was doing all the work so it was decided to make the inside shoulder extremely round and the outside shoulder very sharp. This got the maximum amount of rubber on to the road but allowed a thin round shoulder for running on the straight. Known as the CR81 Mark I (assymetric) this tyre came out in July 1967, initially in 236 compound.

Until there was an improved compound available from a rival manufacturer, this set-up proved the best available equipment for the Mini. But Dunlop were able to gain further improvements with a softer and more ~~stickier~~ version of the 236 compound in 232. At the same time it was felt that there was some loss of stability at higher temperatures and high cornering conditions and this was demonstrated by the peculiar way in which the tyres kept feathering at the edges. So, in November 1967, the CR81 Mark II was introduced in either 236 (for long-distance races) or in 232 (for shorter events).

With the early use of these third generation tyres, the CR81 assymetric on the front meant that the car tended to understeer quite badly and so oversteer was introduced by using the CR70 5·00 L-10 with a tread width of 4½ in. on the rear and on the front of 5¾ in. This, with the power available in those days of around 105 bhp, gave the car reasonably neutral handling.

The 12 in. tyre

It was John Cooper and Ginger Devlin, then manager of the Cooper Mini team, who suggested the fitting of larger diameter wheels way back in 1966 and with the prospects of the Broadspeed Escorts challenging the Minis again in 1969, the matter was once more considered by Dunlop technicians. The Minis were still suffering from lack of adhesion and stability due to high tyre temperatures. The way to improve stability was either to change compound yet again or to increase the contact patch of the tyre which meant more rubber on the road. As it was impossible to go to wider rims because of the ever-present limitations of the homologated bodywork, it was decided to go for the 12 in. diameter rims. This basically enabled the designers to cut the sidewall height by one inch and, by so doing, get higher deflection but maintaining a nice short sidewall which would give good sideways stability. This reduced the general stressing of the cords in the sidewall of the lower profile and it was possible to use a slightly different casing which would, in turn, allow the use of a softer compound.

The first plain tread 12 in. tyre came out in January 1969 and this was the version of the then current Formula I pattern, CR84. It was virtually a racing slick but had the two stage progression effect of the CR81 tread bar block which, when the tyre was half worn, created a very stable pattern. This tyre was first introduced in 236 compound, but there were still problems. With the D15 casing, there was a very rigid sidewall and although the tyre was quite a lot quicker, and it ran cooler, the effect on the car was to make it very reactive to even the slightest twitch of the steering wheel and to bumps and undulations on the road surface. So, in July 1969, the softer 232 compound was introduced and later the more flexible D22 casing.

The move to 12 in. wheels proved that they gave better results when fitted at both front and the rear, rather than with 12 inch at the front and 10 inch at the rear. But so sophisticated now were Mini racing tyres that it became necessary to consider different tyre specifications for different drivers. John Rhodes's driving style was such that he had to have a tyre that was harder and that would tolerate a lot more punishment than other drivers. Gordon Spice, on the other hand, both in the Arden 1000 cc car and the Cooper 1300 cc car, had a lot smoother style and he was able to use the softer 184 compounds.

When the Abingdon team made the switch from rallying to racing in the 1969 season, I at least thought we would be able to forget about the sort of complex tyre plans that we had experienced on the Monte. In fact, the Mini racing scene proved just as confusing. For a typical race meeting during that season, Dunlop would bring along the following equipment for the two-car team – rather more tyres than were demanded by a Formula I team!

10   5·00 L-10 R7 on 5 in. rims for use if the race was to be run on a very wet track

10   CR84 12 in. in 184 compound grooved on 6 in. and 7 in. rims for changeable wet and dry conditions

12   CR84 12 in. in 232 compound on 6 in. and 7 in. rims for normal dry running

6   CR84 12 in. in 236 compound in case ultra high wear was experienced in practice

Finally, for the racing story up to date, Dunlop have since moved on to the fifth generation of Mini tyres by producing a yet wider version of the 10 in. tyre, the CR81 4·50/9·00 – 10. A 2 in. spacer was put into the old 4·50/7·00 mould and the new tyre was originally tried by Coopers on special 8 in. rims. Tests proved that it was highly unstable but at least the tyres ran cool which proved that the whole concept of larger tyres was the answer to the Mini problem.

Although these tyres were not used on international events, because it was impossible to accommodate the wide rims within the homologated bodywork, in 232 and later in 184 compound this tyre has been very successful in club racing.

Rallycross

When in 1969 the Abingdon team started to use the Mini in rally-cross events, a new tyre problem was presented to Dunlop. The Minis were losing out to the rear-wheel-drive cars, and particularly to the rear-engined rear-wheel-drive cars like the Imp. The start, usually on muddy tarmac, was always very important to enable the drivers to get into the first corner ahead of the opposition and thus avoid the flying mud. Chunky tyres which coped well with the mud were far from satisfactory on the tarmac start, particularly with the weight transfer under acceleration on the Mini. The approach was to make a tyre that gave the ultimate grip on the tarmac and try to make it give an acceptable grip on the loose. A 12 in. tyre was used with a very soft compound which gave lots of grip when the tyre was cold. A special tread pattern was designed that helped to squeeze the mud out of the tread. This CR89 pattern was put upon an SP44 type of shoulder with a high stability centre, the centre tread functioning on normal drive grip while the SP44 shoulders coped with the muddy cornering.

In their 15 year association with the team, Dunlop were involved in some 18 major design projects for race and rally tyres for the Mini. Twelve of these, in the course of time, became production tyres that were sold to the public. The cost and the effort involved in each project is formidable for it takes nearly a year for the designer's ideas to be created into a tyre that can be sold over the counter. And one such exercise can cost up to £8,000. But selling competition tyres is a profitable business and Dunlop currently sell at least 3,000 per year of their most popular Mini racing tyres which must help to balance the books.

Just as it is hard to find tangible proof that competition successes sell motor cars, it is even more difficult to say that Dunlop's association with the winning cars sells any more tyres. One can only gain comfort that there is, at the present time, no lack of enthusiasm at Fort Dunlop for support for rallying and saloon car racing, particularly by the big manufacturers.

CHAPTER 11

ANATOMY OF A MONTE

It was Don Morley who once said that to win rallies you need a good car, a good crew, good organization and good luck. To convey something of the organization and behind the scenes work that supported the team's efforts I have reprinted in this chapter the movement schedules and team instructions for the 1968 Monte Carlo Rally.

These are presented word for word as they were issued to the mechanics, drivers and the ice note crews. They contain a lot of detailed information (like travel schedules) which may not be of historical interest but for completeness I have reprinted the whole of what was known as the 'B M C bible'.

I have incorporated some additional explanations where I feel these are necessary to explain certain technicalities which may not be understood by every reader. The original team instructions are in smaller type.

1968 MONTE CARLO RALLY TEAM INSTRUCTIONS

Our wotks entries are as follows:

From Athens	T. Makinen/P. Easter	ORX 77F	No. 7	Mini Cooper 'S' 1275 Gp. II
„ Athens	R. Aaltonen/H. Liddon	ORX 7F	No. 18	„
„ Lisbon	P. Hopkirk/R. Crellin	ORX 777F	No. 87	„
„ Dover	T. Fall/M. Wood	ORX 707F	No. 185	„
„ Dover	B. Culcheth/J. Syer	KOX 391E	No. 172	Austin 1800 Gp. II

Special Tuning have also prepared two 1800's for:

From Dover	J. Sprinzel/G. Ryan	LOF 238F	No. 167	Austin 1800 Gp. II
„ Dover	P. Jopp/W. Cave	LOF 179F	No. 188	„

Team Entries:
Team A   T. Makinen–R. Aaltonen–P. Hopkirk
Team B   A. Fall–B. Culcheth–J. Sprinzel

Service Crews:
Crew A   Princess 'R' (JBL 496D)   W. Price/G. Wiffen
Crew B   Princess 'R' (JBL 492D)   T. Wellman/M. Reade
Crew C   Princess 'R' (NBL 128E)   R. Brown/M. Legg
Crew D   Wolseley (GBL 610C)   N. Hall/J. Weal/B. Moylan
Crew E   Castrol A.60 van   C. Risdon/D. Plummer
Crew F   B M C Van (MJB 442E)   N. Challis/M. Hogan
Crew G   Transporter (B M C 34)   D. Green/R. Whittington/R. Vokins/S.
                                    Bradford
Crew H   Recce Mini   K. Bauman/A. Schultz (B M C Geneva)
N.B. D. Watts will remain at Abingdon and be available to carry out emerg-
ency service.

Ice Note Crews:
Crew A   A. Ambrose/Mrs. B. Ambrose
Crew B   D. Morley/Mrs. V. Morley
Crew C   J. Vernaeve/R. Freeborough
Crew D   G. Mabbs/D. Mabbs

Dunlop Personnel:
   J. Ferguson (Competitions Manager)
   I. Norris (Competitions Press Officer)
   G. Pettinger/F. Smith (Commer van GOM 364D)
   A. Mills/D. Adams (Commer van JOM 509E)
   B. Milcoy/P. Harvey (Commer van 168 MVP)

Castrol Personnel:
   R. Simpson (Competitions Manager)
   J. Simpson, P. Clarke, C. Risdon, R. Stacey, R. Willis, D. Parker

B M C Personnel:
   J. Thornley (Director, MG Car Company – Abingdon)
   R. Baxter (Director, Publicity – Piccadilly)
   A. Zafer (Competitions Press Officer – Abingdon)
   N. Higgins (M G Car Company – Abingdon)
   A. Dawson (B M C Publicity – Longbridge)
   Miss M. Smith (Competitions Department Secretary – Abingdon)

Recce and Practice

Before Christmas 1967 all of the drivers and co-drivers had completed a three weeks recce and practice session covering the Common
Run and the Mountain Circuit.

For the initial recce and making of pace notes they used two completely standard Minis plus two recce Minis (old rally cars) fitted with

standard engines. Standard cars were used for this long and tedious part of the recce because they were both more reliable and more pleasant to drive.

After this first recce, the cars were returned to the BMC agent in Nice, Garage Auber, where with the assistance of one Abingdon mechanic, the two former rally cars were fitted with Group 2 engines. These were brought down to Nice in the back of two new Group 2 recce cars. Thus four Group 2 cars were then available for the final practising session and the two standard cars were available as spares. All of these cars were then left with Garage Auber in Nice to be re-prepared for the use of the ice note crews upon their arrival in Monte.

Pace notes

The use of pace notes, which enable the co-driver to 'talk' his driver corner by corner over special stages, is now an accepted part of the highly professional business of international rallying. No works crew would take their place on the starting ramp today without notes for all of the stages and without having practised those notes as diligently as a racing driver learns his circuits.

Because the sport has become so professional and the international competitions so keen, particularly between manufacturers, it is inevitable that the technique of making and driving on notes (first devised by Tony Ambrose for the Liège in the early 1960s) has been developed (almost entirely by British co-drivers by the way) as a highly sophisticated art. From simple but successful experiments a system of notes written in a special co-driver's shorthand was developed which told the driver how fast he could drive each corner rather than just giving him a physical description of it.

There is obviously a tremendous advantage in being able to pace each corner and to know what lies unseen around the bend. It is difficult to assess how much faster the top crews are when they drive on notes; a lot depends upon the quality of the notes, the experience of the crew and the nature of the stage. Generally, I would estimate that with notes the average works crew would be 15-20% faster than without them.

With normal driving, a considerable part of the driver's concentration will be focused upon reading the road ahead – more difficult, of course, at night than in daytime. With the use of notes he can concentrate completely on driving as fast as he can on the road that he can see and he has the advantage of being able to set the car up correctly, not only for the corner that lies ahead but, more important sometimes, for the one that is out of sight.

The notes should be made in a car with a similar performance to that which will be used for the event. This not only ensures that the pacing of notes is correct, but it also gives the driver practice with the car and it serves as a useful test run for the car. Notes should be made at the same time of day as the stage is to be driven on the event as land marks tend to change with different driving conditions. A seemingly inconspicuous tree trunk by day may stand out like a sore thumb in the glare of quartz headlamps.

The note making would commence with a fairly leisurely run over the whole stage when the driver would call out his gradings, corner by corner. If notes were available from past events, or the co-driver had previously done this groundwork, then this run would be used to check these notes. After this run the crew would return to the start of the test for a second run, slightly faster than the first, with the co-driver now calling back the notes to the driver. There would probably be quite a few corrections to be made as corners are up or down-graded.

This practising would continue until both crew members were completely satisfied that every corner and every hazard was quite perfect and that competitive times were being achieved (bogey times are usually given for the stages). This could take up to 20 runs which over a 70 km stage would mean a couple of nights of really tedious and concentrated work. As the roads would be open to the public, this can be a hazardous business and most crews prefer to make the basic notes by day and practise by night.

Along with developments in the technique of using notes have come improvements in intercom systems which enable the crew to communicate with each other in comfort in the unholy row that goes on inside a rally car in full flight. Today's rally crews use extremely expensive intercom systems built into their crash helmets, a system borrowed from aircraft practice and pioneered by the Morleys on the 1963 Alpine Rally to combat the incredible noise in their 'big Healey'.

The technique of driver and co-driver working with notes demands the highest possible degree of concentration and complete confidence and understanding between the crew. The supreme test of this is driving 'blind' on notes in the fog or mist.

The initial calling of the notes by the driver demands great concentration and practice, particularly as the corner cannot be completely assessed until it has been passed and then the driver must always bear in mind the speed that he anticipated for the approach. Making subsequent corrections to the notes requires a lot of skill and dexterity on the part of the co-driver who not only has to make a legible correction on the move but also has to keep calling the notes.

When calling the notes, the co-driver must get the timing absolutely spot on if the driver is to get the maximum advantage. Reading the notes too fast will mean that the driver has to store up too much information and his concentration will be impaired. Obviously, the driver does not receive the full advantage if the notes are read too slowly. Co-drivers tend to judge their pace by feeling the movements of the car through the seat of their pants rather than risk taking their eyes off the notes to check the road. Perhaps it is no coincidence that most of the best British co-drivers wear half-inch-thick spectacles!

Ice note crews

Pace notes can be made even more effectively with the use of 'ice notes' on events when the road conditions can be changed by weather. This idea was first used on the Monte by the B M C team who co-opted the services of experienced 'retired' rally crews to drive over the stages just before the rally was due to pass. They took with them photo copies of the crews' pace notes and marked the road conditions upon them by underlining the symbols in different colours to denote dry, wet, patchy or solid ice conditions. These notes were then given out to the crews at the start of the test. The advantage of knowing exactly which parts of the stage were dry and which were ice covered made a dramatic difference to the stage times and this work undoubtedly contributed a lot to B M C's Monte wins. From these notes, of course, the crews were also able to make a very accurate choice of tyres – vitally important on the Monte.

DRIVERS' TRAVEL TO STARTS

Wednesday 17 January: T. Makinen/P. Easter and R. Aaltonen/H. Liddon fly Nice–Rome (flight AZ.339) depart 13.55 arrive 15.10, then Rome–Athens (flight AZ.744) depart 16.20, arrive 19.00. Accommodation booked Olympic Palace, Filellinon Street.

P. Hopkirk/R. Crellin fly Nice–Lisbon (Pan American 155) depart 10.35, arrive 13.55. Accommodation booked Hotel Fenix, Praca Marques de Pombal.

Thursday 18 January: T. Fall/M. Wood fly Nice–London (flight BE.105) depart 14.45, arrive 15.30, met at airport. Collect rally car from Abingdon and make their own way to the Dover start. B. Culcheth/J. Syer collect 1800 from Abingdon and make their own way to the Dover start.

Rooms for T. Fall/M. Wood and B. Culcheth/J. Syer booked from noon on the 19th at the Dover Stage Hotel.

ICE NOTE CREWS TRAVEL TO MONTE

Saturday 20 January: D. Morley and Mrs. Morley fly London–Nice (flight BE.104) depart 10.45, arrive 13.30 A. Ambrose and Mrs. Ambrose, R. Freeborough, G. Mabbs and D. Mabbs fly London–Paris (flight AF.807) depart 09.30, arrive 11.30, then Paris–Nice (flight AF.024) depart 12.10. arrive 13.25. Take taxi to Garage Auber, collect four best recce Minis and drive to Monte.

J. Vernaeve makes his own way to Monte from Ghent by car to arrive by the morning of Saturday 20 January.

SERVICE CREWS TRAVEL TO STARTS

Monday 8 January: D. Green, R. Whittington, R. Vokins and S. Bradford with Transporter (BMC 34) carrying two Minis (ORX 7F and ORX 77F) cross Southampton–Le Havre, depart 23.00, arrive 07.00 (9th), cabins booked: Drive to Brindisi (1,300 miles). D. Green and R. Whittington with two Minis cross Brindisi–Patras on Monday 15 January, depart 23.00, arrive 18.00 (16th). Drive to Athens to arrive by Wednesday, 17th January. Transporter with R. Vokins and S. Bradford drive to Padora (550 miles) to service rally *en route* to Monte.

Friday 12 January: W. Price and G. Wiffen with Princess 'R' (JBL 496D) and trailer carrying Mini (ORX 777F) cross Southampton–Le Havre, depart 23.00, arrive 07.00 (13th), cabins booked. Drive to Lisbon (1,100 miles) to arrive during Wednesday 17 January.

Thursday 18 January: P. Browning, A. Zafer and Miss M. Smith fly London–Nice (flight BE 104) depart 10.45, arrive 13.30. Take taxi to Monte.

N. Challis/M. Hogan with van (MJB 442E) cross Southampton–Le Havre, depart 23.00, arrive 07.00 (19th).

Saturday 20 January: T. Wellman/M. Reade/D. Plummer with Princess 'R' (JBL 492D), R. Brown/M. Legg with Princess 'R' (NBL 128E) and N. Hall/J. Weal/B. Moylan with Wolseley (GBL 610C) travel to Dover. D. Plummer joins C. Risdon with Castrol A.60 van at Dover and all cross Dover–Boulogne with rally cars, depart 02.30, arrive 05.00.

K. Bauman and A. Schultz (BMC Dealers, Geneva) drive from Geneva to arrive in Monte by Sunday 21 January.

LOADING FOR SERVICE CARS

3 Princess 'R's, 1 Wolseley

Full Mini kits and running repair kits for 1800. One small Mini and 1800 running repair kit to be taken to Dover by one car and handed over to Castrol A.60 van (Risdon/Plummer).

Van

Full Mini kit and 1800 running repair kit for own use. Two small Mini kits to be handed on to B. Whittington and K. Bauman / A. Schultz service cars in Monte. One full 1800 kit and Mini running repair kit to be handed on to B. Moylan / D. Plummer 1800 service car in Monte. Four standard seats with covers to be exchanged for full recliners on arrival at Monte. Balance of fuel bags. One fuel drum and pump.

Transporter

One full Mini kit to cover Athens–Monte service points. One full Mini kit to be handed over to R. Stacey at Brindisi to cover Athens–Monte service points

General

All service vehicles to carry Mini quick lift jacks, hydrolastic pumps, welding gear. Cars should carry four fuel bags each to Monte, the balance will be carried in the van and handed out before the Monte–Vals–Monte leg and the Mountain Circuit as per fuel plans.

START POINTS TO MONTE SERVICE SCHEDULE

Time of First Car	Point	Crew	Car
20 January			
01.30	Dover	Hall/Weal/Moylan	Wolseley
13.26	Boulogne (2nd time)	Wellman/Read	Princess 'R'
10.00	Brussels	V. Vernaeve	Mini, 1100
10.35	Madrid	Price/Wiffen	Princess 'R'
17.32	Belgrade	Green/Whittington/Stacey	A.60
21.55	Bayonne	Price/Wiffen	Princess 'R'
23.40	Poitiers	Hall/Weal/Moylan	Wolseley
21 January			
02.15	Bergerac	Brown/Legg	Princess 'R'
07.49	Millau	Risdon/Plummer	Castrol A.60
14.38	S. Flour	Brown/Legg	Princess 'R'
18.58	Padova	Vokins/Bradford	Transporter
20.20	Bourg	Dunlop	Transporter
21.28	Trento	Green/Whittington/Stacey	A.60
21.42	S. Claud	Hall/Weal/Moylan	Wolseley
22 January			
03.14	Alessandria	Vokins/Bradford	Transporter
05.11	Digne	Risdon/Plummer	Castrol A.60
08.13	Monte	Wellman/Reade	Princess 'R'
		Challis/Hogan	Van
		Price/Wiffen	Princess 'R'

NOTES ON SERVICE FROM START TO MONTE

1. Times shown on the service schedule are for the time of arrival of the first car. At most points, however, cars could be 20–30 minutes early.

2. The service cars at Monte will remove the roof racks from the Minis and replace the full reclining passenger seats with standard Mini seats and covers.

3. If service crews could organize a room and washing facilities at hotels near to service points this would be useful in case the crews have a lot of time in hand.

4. Refuelling and servicing on the public highway is prohibited on all itineraries between the arrival and departure points in Monaco and the towns of Menton and La Turbie. However, the organizers confirm that as in previous years servicing can be carried out in garages *off the public highway*. When the cars first arrive in Monte (and after the Monte–Vals–Monte leg) service will be at Esso Service Buckel, Moyenne Corniche, Cap d'Ail (tel. Cap d'Ail 82.23.80).

5. A. M. Almeida Comercio of Lisbon (tel. 320319) and Doucas in Athens (tel. 912.029) have been asked to provide garaging and servicing facilities at the start.

6. B M C Garages have been asked to provide service at the following points and display B M C signs: *Athens start* Larissa, Cuneo; *Lisbon start* Zaragova, Pamplona; *Dover start* Lille, Ostende, Auriac.
   If crews have time in hand and don't need service please stop and say hello to these people so that they will be encouraged to help us again in the future.

7. If the car is in trouble on the run to Monte drivers or mechanics should phone D. Watts in England (Abingdon 1946) who will fly out with spares to intercept the Rally.

8. It is prohibited for any competitor to park or stop on the highway or the roadside at a distance of less than 100 metres from a time or passage control or an arrival or starting point of the classification test. Mechanics must watch this point and as a general rule work before controls. On the Monte–Vals–Monte leg and the Mountain Circuit mechanics must be prepared to run through the control and work on the other side as well if necessary.

9. D. Green and R. Whittington will have to get the two Minis transferred from their passports on to those of the drivers.

10. D. Plummer to travel to Dover with T. Wellman/M. Reade to meet C. Risdon of Castrol (A.60 van). Take small Mini running repair kit and transfer this to the A.60 at Dover.

11. B. Moylan/D. Plummer to collect 1800 (LMO 391E) from Garage Auber on arrival at Monte and load their service kit which will be carried down in the van.

12. All barges to Monte will carry $2 \times \frac{3}{4}$ studs.

FUEL PLANS FOR MONTE–VALS–MONTE LEG

Because of the very tight time schedules on the Common Run and the Mountain Circuit there is not time for the Rally cars to refuel at garages. Service crews therefore have to provide fuel from full bags (capacity 4 gallons) or from special fuel drums.

Fuel for $4 \times$ Minis and 1×1800

Place	Bags per car	Total bags	Crew
P. des Moilans	4 gallons from drum	20 gallons from drum	F
S. Auban	$1\frac{1}{2}$	7	G
Les Grillons	$1\frac{1}{2}$	7	A
Chamloc	2	10	C
S. Agreve	3	15	B
Burzet (1st time)	$1\frac{1}{2}$	7	D
Burzet (2nd time)	—	—	D
Vals les Bains	2	10	H
Aubenas	2	10	E
Bedoin	2	10	A
Orpiere	2	10	G
Gap	$1\frac{1}{2}$	7	C
Selonnet	6 gallons from drum	30 gallons from drum	F
Digne	2	10	B
Montferrat	2	10	A
P. C. Albert	1	5	E
Levens	$1\frac{1}{2}$	7	G
Monte	(see note below)		C + D

Crew	Total bags carried	Total fills
A	10	$7 + 10 + 10 = 27$
B	15	$15 + 10 = 25$
C	10	$10 + 7 = 17$
D	7	7
E	10	$10 + 5 = 15$
F	1 drum	50 gallons
G	10	$7 + 10 + 7 = 24$
H	10	10
	$\overline{72}$	

If P. Browning has been unable to arrange the Monte service point at a garage, crews C and D should each bring all their bags full. This to be advised at the final briefing.

SERVICE POINTS MOUNTAIN CIRCUIT

TIME	PLACE	POINT	CREW	CAR
25 January				
19.13	Menton	Emergency	Moylan/Plummer	1800
19.36	Sospel	Control Start Stage 1	Wellman/Brown/Bradford	Princess 'R'
19.51	Moulinet	End Stage 1, Start Stage 2	Hall/Vokins/Weal	Wolseley
20.16	La Bollene	End Stage 2	Bauman/Schultz	Mini
20.42	Le Chaudan	Control	Price/Wiffen/Legg	Princess 'R'
21.16	St. Sauveur	Control Start Stage 3	Green/Reade	Princess 'R'
21.38	Beuil	End Stage 3	Whittington/Auber mex	Mini
22.11	Puget-Theniers	Control	Challis/Hogan	Van
23.21	Levens	Control	Moylan/Plummer	1800
23.50	La Bollene	Start Stage 4	Bauman/Schultz	Mini
26 January				
00.15	Moulinet	End Stage 4	Hall/Vokins/Weal	Wolseley
00.30	Sospel	Control	Wellman/Brown/Bradford	Princess 'R'
01.38	D414/N202	Control	Price/Wiffen/Legg	Princess 'R'
02.28	St. Sauveur	Control Start Stage 5	Green/Reade	Princess 'R'
02.51	Beuil	End Stage 5	Whittington/Auber mex	Mini
03.23	Puget-Theniers	Control	Challis/Hogan	Van
04.33	Levens	Control	Moylan/Plummer	1800
05.02	La Bollene	Start Stage 6	Bauman/Schultz	Mini
05.27	Moulinet	End Stage 6	Hall/Vokins/Weal	Wolseley
05.42	Sospel	Control	Wellman/Brown/Bradford	Princess 'R'
06.19	Monte	Control	Price/Wiffen/Legg	Princess 'R'

Possible time in hand will be given to mechanics at the final briefing; generally most service points will be racing pit stops.

FUEL PLANS FOR MOUNTAIN CIRCUIT

Fuel for 4 × Minis, 1 × 1800

Place	Available per car	Total available	Crew
Sospel	$\frac{1}{2}$ bag (emerg.)	2 bags	B
Moulinet	$\frac{1}{2}$ bag (emerg.)	2 bags	D
La Bollene	1 bag	5 bags	H
Le Chaudan	$1\frac{1}{2}$ bags	7 bags	A
St. Sauveur	1 bag	5 bags	C
Beuil	$\frac{1}{2}$ bag (emerg.)	2 bags	G
Puget-Theniers	6 galls from drum	30 galls. drum	F

Place	Available per car	Total available	Crew
Levens	1 bag	5 bags	E
La Bollene (2nd time)	½ bag	2½ bags	H
Moulinet (2nd time)	½ bag (emerg.)	2 bags	D
Sospel (2nd time)	2 bags	10 bags	B
D414/N202	1½ bags	7 bags	A
St. Sauveur (2nd time)	1 bag	5 bags	C
Beuil (2nd time)	½ bag (emerg.)	2 bags	G
Puget-Theniers (2nd time)	6 galls from drum	30 galls drum	F
Levens (2nd time)	1 bag	5 bags	E
La Bollene (3rd time)	½ bag	2½ bags	H
Moulinet (3rd time)	½ bag (emerg.)	2 bags	D
Sospel (3rd time)	1 bag	5 bags	B

Crew	Total bags carried	Total fills
A	7	7 + 7 = 14
B	17	2 + 10 + 5 = 17
C	10	5 + 5 = 10
D	6	2 + 2 + 2 = 6
E	10	5 + 5 = 10
F	2 bags + drum	30 + 30 = 60 galls.
G	4	2 + 2 = 4
H	10	5 + 2½ + 2½ = 10
	66	

Crews A, B and F should be able to refuel at the Garage between the first and second circuits.

Crew F should always have two bags at the ready in case two cars arrive at the same time and are unable to fill from the drum.

NOTES FOR ICE NOTE CREWS

1. When you arrive in Monte, go to Garage Auber and collect the four best recce Minis. Pick the best selection of tyres and make sure that you have a reasonable running repair kit, some tools and at least one petrol bag on board.

2. Check with Garage Auber to see whether the crews have left their pace notes there. If they are not there they will be at the Helder.

3. Come to the Helder, meet P. Browning, collect your pace notes and any final instructions. You should leave Monte during Saturday afternoon.

4. With so many tyres and so many options available this year, road reports are going to be very useful as a guide to Dunlops as to which are the most likely tyres to be used at the various points. Generally all the Dunlop vans will have available all the options, but they will only have sufficient wheels to offer about five options per car. Your road reports will therefore serve as Dunlops fitting up instructions.

5. Miss M. Smith will be on 24-hour phone duty at the Helder (tel. to be advised) to receive your road reports. You should give your first report

on Sunday afternoon, followed by reports on Monday morning, on Monday afternoon and throughout Monday night. A final report on Tuesday morning would be useful.

6. We will have our own weather forecasting service in operation and Miss Smith will be able to give you local forecasts.

7. The Dunlop crews will phone the Helder to receive information regarding your road reports. When you call at the Helder on Saturday afternoon it is hoped that we can give you details regarding time and place for a rendezvous with the Dunlop crews in your area so that you can pass on your reports direct.

8. The crews will have written their pace notes to agree page by page with H. Liddon's master notes. (They have also been asked, where possible, to write their notes to agree line by line with the master notes.) This should assist with the ice note marking.

9. Notes should be marked as follows: underlined in yellow means road wet; underlined in dotted red means patchy ice or snow; underlined in solid red means ice and snow.

INSTRUCTIONS FOR ICE NOTE CREWS, MONTE–VALS–MONTE LEG

Note: Some of the less important road reporting will be covered by the service cars on their way to their service points.

Crew A   A. Ambrose / Mrs. Ambrose (covering Tests 1 and 6)
Do road report from Monte along the route over Test 1 (S. Auban) to junction N211/N85. Give road reports on this section; do ice notes for Test 1 and hand these out at the start of Test 1.
After passage of the Rally go to Test 6 (Chorges) over the route in the reverse direction from Digne and give road reports on this section. Do ice notes for Test 6 and hand these out at the start of Test 6. Go to the end of Test 6 after Makinen and Aaltonen, and get their comments to pass on to Hopkirk and Fall. Return to Monte after the passage of the Rally.

Crew B   D. Morley / Mrs. Morley (covering Tests 2, 3 and 7)
Go direct to S. Agreve and cover the route from here over Test 2 and over Test 3 to Vals-les-Bains. Give road reports over this section, do the ice notes for both Tests and hand them out at S. Agreve. Establish a phone contact between Burzet and S. Agreve so that latest reports from Burzet can be passed back. Burzet also to phone back reports from Makinen and Aaltonen for the benefit of Hopkirk and Fall.
After the passage of the Rally go direct to Test 7 (Levens), do the ice notes for this Test and hand them out at the start of the Test.
Return to Monte after the passage of the Rally.

Crew C   J. Vernaeve / R. Freeborough (covering Test 4)
Go direct to Bedoin and cover the road reporting from here to Orpiere and over Test 4 (Col de Perty). Give road reports over this section, do the ice notes for Test 4 and issue these at the start of Test 4.
Return to Monte after the passage of the Rally.

Crew D　G. Mabbs | D. Mabbs (covering Test 5)

Go direct to Test 5 (Gap), do the ice notes for this test and hand them out at the start of the Test. Go to Gap after Makinen and Aaltonen are through and get their comments to pass on to Hopkirk and Fall.

Return to Monte after the passage of the Rally.

INSTRUCTIONS FOR ICE NOTE CREWS, MOUNTAIN CIRCUIT

All four crews should leave Monte early morning on Thursday.

J. Vernaeve / R. Freeborough to concentrate exclusively on ice notes for Test 1, 2, 4 and 6 (Turini) handing these out at Sospel first time through. Advise Dunlop crew at Sospel of most likely tyre requirements and phone reports back to Helder throughout the day. Assist with service at Sospel.

G. Mabbs / D. Mabbs do road reporting *en route* east of a line Nice to S. Sauveur. Advise Dunlop crews at all controls of likely tyre requirements and phone reports back to Helder. Generally float around in this area during the passage of the Rally to assist with service.

D. Morley / Mrs Morley to concentrate exclusively on ice notes for Tests 3 and 5 (S. Sauveur). Establish phone contact between Garage at Beuil and S. Sauveur so that after Makinen and Aaltonen have been through their reports can be passed back for information of Hopkirk and Fall. Advise Dunlop crews at S. Sauveur of likely tyre requirements and phone reports back to Helder throughout the day. Assist with service at S. Sauveur and if possible try and do a run over the Test between the first and second crossings.

A. Ambrose / Mrs. Ambrose do road reporting on route west of a line Nice to S. Sauveur. Advise Dunlop crews at all controls of likely tyre requirements and phone reports back to Helder. Generally float around in this area during the passage of the Rally to assist with service.

MONTE-VALS-MONTE LEG, ROAD REPORTING BY SERVICE CREWS

The following service crews are asked to phone Miss Smith at the Helder (tel. to be advised) with a report of road conditions on the way to their service points on the Monte-Vals-Monte leg.

D. Green / M. Reade to report on the road conditions along the Rally route from junction N211/N85 to Chamaloc.

T. Wellman / R. Brown / S. Bradford to report on the road conditions from Chamaloc over the Col de Rousset and along the Rally route to S. Agreve.

B. Moylan / D. Plummer to report on the road conditions from Bedoin along the Rally route in the reverse direction to Aubenas.

C. Bauman / A. Schultz to cover the section Vals-les-Bains to Aubenas and report the road conditions.

GENERAL NOTES

1. Works crews who retire will be expected to assist with service or ice note work later in the event.
2. All fuel bags carried on Rally cars will be handed over to service crews on arrival at Monte.
3. Abingdon service crews will use their normal octagon signs. Dealers *en route* to Monte have been asked to display B M C signs.
4. It is the co-driver's responsibility to say how long can be spared at service points, to say what work is to be done and how much time there is in hand. In view of the large permutation of tyres available please be specific about your requirements and appreciate that the mechanics will not be as familiar as you are with recognizing the tyres.
5. Service crews should consult the co-drivers in Monte over the most suitable places to set up their service points on the Monte–Vals–Monte leg and the Mountain Circuit.
6. Mechanics must study the fuel plans carefully in conjunction with the service schedules. Watch the fire risk with the inevitable spectators and always have a fire extinguisher at hand.
7. The four works Minis will always have preference for servicing over the 1800. The two Special Tuning 1800s should be given full works service if there's time and providing the supply of spares does not jeopardize the chances of Culcheth/Syer. Help private owners only if you have time.
8. The Culcheth/Syer 1800 will be running on a special mineral oil. This will be provided in plain Castrol tins marked B204. Each service car will carry at least one gallon tin.
9. On the way to their first service point on the Monte–Vals–Monte leg, W. Price/G. Wiffen/M. Legg collect the B M C transporter from Dunlops in Monte and drive it to the nearest garage to the control at Pont Charles Albert. Lock the transporter and leave the keys with the garage. These will be picked up by B. Moylan/D. Plummer when they arrive to cover this service point. There will be no Dunlop crew here so B. Moylan/D. Plummer assisted by D. Morley and D. Parker (Castrol) will have to unload the transporter and have all tyres sorted. B. Moylan to bring the transporter back to Dunlops in Monte afterwards.
10. There should be no late night revelry until the Mountain Circuit is over!
11. Remember that our cars will be bunched closer together for the Mountain Circuit. An order of priority for work will be given at the final mechanics briefing.
12. Mechanics will be given their petrol money at the first mechanics briefing.
13. On the Monte–Vals–Monte leg service cars should leave immediately the five works cars and the two Special Tuning 1800s are through.
14. On the Mountain Circuit most service crews see the Rally through several times at the same place. Study the routes so that you know from which direction to expect the cars.
15. On arrival at Monte for the first time all service crews should check over their kits and make sure that they have the correct number of fuel bags

according to the fuel plans. Crews must do the same before the Mountain Circuit.

16. All mechanics must be at meetings at The Helder at *18.00 hrs. on Monday 22nd* and at *18.00 hrs on Wednesday 24th*.

17. We have three electric impact drills to be used for wheel changing. For the Monte–Vals–Monte leg these should be carried by Wellman/Brown/ Bradford, Hall/Vokins/Weal and Moylan/Plummer. For the Mountain Circuit they should be carried by Wellman/Brown/Bradford, Green/ Reade and Bauman/Schultz.

TYRES

As we have more tyres on this year's Monte than ever before, and no less than 13 permutations of tread pattern and studding, it is absolutely essential that everyone is thoroughly familiar with what the tyres look like and what they are called.

The following is a list of all the tyres available:

R7 Green spot racers
CR70 Green spot racers
SP44 Dry compound, plain (un-studded)
SP44 Wet compound, plain (un-studded)
SP3 Studded
SP44 Dry compound, part-stud, graded
SP44 Wet compound, part-stud, graded
SP44 three-quarter studded, graded
SP44 Full stud, graded
SP44 Full stud, non-graded
Chisels (long and short versions)
Knobs (long and short versions)
'Hakka' specials

Graded tyres have their studs protruding at varying lengths in the tread pattern. These tyres are also studded with a greater number of studs in the trailing block of the tread pattern, thus graded tyres are 'directional' and have to be fitted on the correct side of the car.

To facilitate fitting tyres will be colour coded as follows:

All dry compound tyres will be painted BLUE.
All wet compound tyres will be painted GREEN.
Graded tyres with RED flash must be fitted to off-side of car.
Graded tyres with YELLOW flash must be fitted to near-side of car.

(Tyre fitters will have to ensure that the colour flash appears on the *outside* of the wheel when the tyre is fitted.)

TRAVEL HOME

Sunday 28 January: 2 recce Minis, 4 rally Minis, 1 rally 1800, 3 barges, 1 service 1800 plus 10 mechanics, A. Zafer, B. Culcheth, J. Syer, P. Easter, G. Mabbs, D. Mabbs and R. Freeborough take Monaco–Boulogne train, depart 16.30 arrive 08.30 on 29 January. Cross Boulogne–Dover, depart 12.00, arrive 12.30

S. Bradford and R. Vokins with transporter carrying 2 recce Minis, N. Challis and M. Hogan with van, W. Price and G. Wiffen with barge and trailer carrying one Mini drive to Boulogne (715 miles) and cross Boulogne-Dover on Tuesday 30 January, depart 12.00, arrive 12.30.

K. Bauman and A. Schultz take two standard recce Minis back to Geneva. P. Browning, R. Aaltonen, T. Fall, M. Wood, H. Liddon, P. Hopkirk, Miss M. Smith, Mr. & Mrs. A. Ambrose, Mr. & Mrs. Morley fly Nice–Paris (flight AF 017) depart 14.30, arrive 15.50, then Paris–London (flight AF 822) depart 17.00, arrive 18.00.

T. Makinen flies Nice–Frankfurt (flight LH 363) depart 17.15, arrive 19.20, then Frankfurt–Helsinki (flight AY 824) depart 20.25, arrive 23.45 on Sunday 28 January.

If we win, the above schedule will be re-arranged to include on the charter flight home as many of the team cars as we can get on the plane, all the drivers. the mechanics who built the winning car and as many others as possible.

Post Mortem

After every event the crews were asked to complete and return a report form covering all aspects of the car's performance and the general team organization. These forms were not only circulated within the Department but were also sent to the Heads of Departments in B M C and to all the supporting trade personnel as applicable. The following report is by Tony Fall and Mike Wood for the 1968 Monte.

COMPETITION REPORT FORM

Type of car: Mini Cooper 'S' 1275 Mk. II Reg. No. ORX 707F. Group: 2. Event: Monte 1968. Date: 19–26 January. Driver: T. Fall. Co-driver: M. Wood. Approximate mileage covered: 4,750 km.

I.   ENGINE

Power satisfactory?	Yes
Carburation and ignition satisfactory?	Flat spot on carbs when braking
Petrol consumption?	Approximately 180 km. per fill-up
Oil consumption?	Negligible
Grade of oil?	Castrol XXL
Oil pressure variation?	Nil
Any oil surge?	No
Max. revs used?	8,000 rpm
Any excessive pinking or running-on experienced?	No
Any overheating?	Yes, when reaching the top of the Turini we overheated (100°C) with apparent loss of power

Any work carried out?   Carbs retuned at St. Sauveur by Den Green

2. TRANSMISSION

Any noise?	Normal
Any vibration?	Yes. Drone at certain revs
Ease of change?	Very good
Clutch satisfactory?	Yes. Clutch slave cylinder replaced
Gearbox and final drive ratios satisfactory?	Yes

3. SUSPENSION AND ROADHOLDING

How was the general balance
of the car?   Very good – the best yet with anti-roll bar
                               fitted. Please fit to all future rally cars –
                               except for very rough events

How was the steering?   Very good
Type of tyres fitted?   Racers and full popins non-graded
No. of tyre changes?   Don't know
What was the tyre wear and
what pressures?   Wear normal. 40 lb front, 35 lb rear
Any road wheel trouble?   No
Any shock absorber trouble?   No
Any hydrolastic trouble?   No
Number of times suspension
pressurized?   None

4. BRAKING

Brake material used?   Ferodo DS.11 front, VG.95 rear
Pedal pressure satisfactory?   Yes. A 425 lb per sq in. limiting valve was
                               fitted. Please always fit this specification on
                               my future rally cars. For my style of driving
                               this proved very satisfactory.

Did you experience brake fade
and under what conditions?   No
Did you experience any
serious wheel locking?   No
How often were the brakes
adjusted?   Twice
How often was brake material
renewed?   Once

5. ELECTRICAL SYSTEM

Was the lighting satisfactory? Yes
Did you have any fanbelt
trouble?   Tightened once
Was the intercom satisfactory? Very good but tended to fade after much use

Did you make any electrical repairs or replacements?

One fuse kept repeatedly blowing. This was when we used the centre spot lamps through the dip switch. It was OK when we used them direct

6. BODY

Were there any leaks or draughts?

No

Was the seating satisfactory?

Yes. Please always use drivers' seat brackets on my future rally cars

Type of seats fitted?

Full recliners to Monte then lightweight seats

Were the switches and minor controls in easy places?

Yes

Were the seat belts satisfactory?

Yes

Make and type of seat belts fitted?

Irvin full harness

Did the screen wipers and washers work satisfactorily?

New Trico washers very good

Was the heating, demisting and ventilation effective?

Yes

Were the instruments accurate, visible and well lit at night?

The rev counter was way out

Were rally clocks accurate?

Rally clocks again failed half-way

7. PREPARATION

Was the car handed over to you in good condition?

Yes

Were travel arrangements satisfactory?

Yes

Were the tools, spares and equipment sufficient and satisfactory?

Yes

Was hotel accommodation satisfactory?

Yes

Were the servicing arrangements during event adequate?

The best yet – after the pep talk at the end of the Common Run!

How did your car compare with its rally or commercial competitors?

Not fast enough to beat a Porsche!

CHAPTER 12

LUCKLESS YEAR

The Monte plans described in the previous chapter ran completely to form and nobody could have asked for more dedicated efforts by drivers, co-drivers, mechanics and supporting trade personnel. The only thing that did not go to plan was the weather, for 1968 brought the first of the freak 'no snow' years which started the Porsche domination.

Under these conditions the Minis were completely handicapped out of the running against the growing competition from Alpine-Renault and Porsche. While front-wheel-drive gave a certain advantage on the snow and ice, particularly on the downhill sections, the advantage swung dramatically to rear-engined rear-wheel-drive cars on the drier going. Furthermore, the performance of the new generation of sports/racers now put the Minis a long way behind on performance.

Although the results of the 1968 event were disappointing, everyone realized that in the circumstances we could not have achieved a better result. Rauno Aaltonen, Tony Fall and Paddy Hopkirk finished third, fourth and fifth overall in that order behind the Porsches. They won the Team Prize and were placed 1-2-3 in the class. Timo Makinen's car was the only one to have any trouble when the crankshaft pulley came loose. He arrived at Monte with a white-hot engine and failed to re-start for the Mountain Circuit.

I say that everything went according to plan on the 1968 Monte. That was not exactly so because this was the year of the carburetter controversy that very nearly caused as much of a rumpus as those quartz iodine lights in 1966. For the first time we were using the twin split-Weber carburetters in Group 2, developed and built by Abingdon from prototypes that Timo Makinen had seen in Finland. Basically by cutting a pair of standard Weber carburetters in half and fitting the two left-hand 'halves' on to the standard Group 2 inlet manifold, it was possible to gain Group 6 Weber type performance in Group 2 (an advantage of some 7 bhp).

Having studied the Group 2 regulations very carefully I was confident that the use of these carburetters was permissible. Nevertheless, I wrote to the FIA in Paris and to the Monte organizers many weeks before the event sending them details and photographs of our new carburetters. They thus had ample opportunity to raise any queries and, to indicate that we had no intentions of cheating, we passed on details of the new engine specification to the press. Nobody said anything about it until we arrived in Monte!

After the Concentration Runs I was asked to attend a meeting of the Sporting Commission, for following the initial technical examination of the cars upon arrival in Monte Carlo, the Technical Commission had informed the Sporting Commission that they had doubts about the eligibility of the carburetters. They wished to discuss my interpretation of the regulations covering this point.

It was clear from the start that they were doing this in a genuine attempt to safeguard BMC and the Rally from a repetition of the 1966 fiasco when they were aware of the infringement of the regulations at an early stage in the Rally and yet they permitted the Minis to finish the event before disqualifying them. I was told that there was no doubt that a protest would be forthcoming from other competitors if we continued using the new carburetters and they wanted to discuss the matter at the earliest opportunity. I began by thanking them for the opportunity of this early discussion and we were agreed that for the good of the Monte and rallying in general we should do everything possible to prevent a repetition of the 1966 happenings.

The English translation of the French regulations covering the alterations permitted to carburetters says 'The carburetters provided by the manufacturer may be replaced by others of a different size providing that the number be the same as that provided by the manufacturer and that they can be mounted on the inlet manifold of the engine without using any intermediary device and by using the original attachment parts'.

The Technical Commission began by suggesting that we had fitted 'an intermediary device' between the carburetters and the manifold. I replied that this was not 'an intermediary device' but an integral part of the carburetter. I explained that this was a prototype carburetter which, according to my interpretation of the regulations, began at the point of junction with the manifold and continued through the main body of the carburetter to the end of the inlet pipe. I pointed out that the small additional inlet stub on the carburetter was not bolted to the carburetter but was welded to it as a complete unit.

While the Sporting Commission were clearly divided over this point, the original French text of the regulations was read and it was found that there was a discrepancy between the English and French texts. In the French text the interpretation of the final wording of the regulations reads 'the carburetters must be mounted on the inlet manifold of the engine *without modification or deformation* and without using any intermediary device, and by using the original attachment parts'. The words in italics were omitted from the English text.

While the Sporting Commission was clearly very concerned about the discrepancy in the text on a very significant matter, we agreed that only the French text could be accepted as the official code. The Commission then felt that the carburetters were not eligible because we had modified them to make them fit the standard manifold. Again I pointed out that we had not modified them because, although we had used basic Weber principles and some design features and components, this was an entirely new prototype carburetter which we had designed and built in England. There could, therefore, be no question that we had modified them to make them fit the manifold; they were designed to fit the manifold in the first place. After one hour the meeting was adjourned for the Technical Commission to make its decision.

I was later asked to rejoin the meeting and the verdict of the Technical Commission was that in the event of a protest they felt that they would have to uphold it as they were still not satisfied that the carburetters were in accordance with the regulations. In view of the fact that we had discussed matters in such a friendly and frank atmosphere and, bearing in mind the discrepancy of English and French texts, they were prepared to offer us the opportunity of changing the carburetters before the Monte-Vals-Monte leg. I said that this would be quite impossible because, even if our crews could make up enough time to have the work done, we had not got any S U carburetters with us. Furthermore, I said that I thought it would be a scandalous thing to do which would give rise to a lot more protests from our competitors. It was also putting the organizers into an even more embarrassing position who, having allowed us to start, now wanted us to 'secretly' change the specification of our engines.

The atmosphere was now getting somewhat strained and the Commission then offered us the opportunity of changing the carburetters in *parc ferme*! This proposal was even more stupid than the first and I reminded them that the whole purpose of our

discussion was to try and avoid a repetition of 1966 and not to create an
even bigger fiasco! The atmosphere of the meeting was clearly demonstrated when I was then presented with what was clearly a bogus tele-
phone message reporting that Paddy Hopkirk was in the *parc ferme* at this
very moment trying to change his carburetters! What had I got to
say about that? I looked across the table at the RAC Steward, Jack
Kemsley, in sheer amazement and said that if this were so then I suggest
that we all go down to the *parc ferme* right away to witness that
Paddy was as good a mechanic as a driver! My humour was not appreciated but I think we won that round as the matter was quickly
forgotten. Continuing the argument, I was adamant that our cars
complied with whatever translation of the regulations one chose. I
again refused to change the carburetters and in such a clearly hostile
atmosphere I said that I must now consider withdrawing the team.

Following long discussions with the drivers, opinions were divided
as to whether they should stick their necks out on the Common Run
and the Mountain Circuit only to face the chance of disqualification
or withdraw now and save the cars for another more worthwhile
event. It was a difficult decision and it was by no means unanimous
that, after yet another meeting with the Technical Commission, we
decided to press on. The final meeting had at least indicated that the
Monte organizers would not raise any objections or disqualify us but
they would have to carefully consider the reasons presented by anyone
who lodged an official protest. This, we thought, would be the end of
the matter because it was clear that all of our rivals agreed with our
interpretation of the regulations.

With the Rally over, the cars were taken to the usual scrutineering
but our suspicions were aroused when instead of asking for just the
class-winning car, the scrutineers demanded to see all three Minis.
Heading the scrutineering team was the same gentleman who had
been officiating in 1966 and clearly he was still very anti-B M C and
he certainly did not agree with the Sporting Commission's decision
that the carburetters complied with the regulations.

The carburetters and manifolds were torn apart to try and find
some slight discrepancy with the regulations or the homologation
sheet. It was a brain-washing but unsuccessful exercise that took so
long that, by the time the scrutineers' lunchtime came around and he
shut up shop, there was not time even to take a cursory glance over
the winning Porsche!

After the promises made by the Commission I'm afraid I came away from the Monte that year wondering how they have the cheek to call their organizing body the 'Sporting Commission'. The matter was finally resolved by sending formal application to the FIA who ultimately agreed that our interpretation of the regulations was correct and that the carburetters were eligible.

For the rest of the 1968 season, the troubles and disappointments can fairly be blamed on bad luck, although undoubtedly many of the retirements – and there were lots of them – could be attributed to the fact that the Minis were now being considerably overstressed to keep pace with the opposition. While in 1967 reliability had often won through, with the demand for more power to keep pace with the Porsche opposition, the Minis now added unreliability to a non-competitive performance on many events.

Undoubtedly another reason for the lack of Mini success was that a great deal of Abingdon's time was now being directed to the testing and development of the 1800 in preparation for the *Daily Express* London-to-Sydney Marathon to be held at the end of the year. This meant, particularly in the latter part of the season, that there was a complete stop on all Mini development and testing at a time when it was most necessary.

There was therefore very little to shout about in 1968, with the exception of a good Tulip Rally performance by Julian Vernaeve (third overall) and a fine performance on the Scottish Rally by Lars Ytterbring who finished a close runner-up to Roger Clark's Escort Twin Cam. Paddy Hopkirk led the Canadian Shell 4000 Rally for three days and then had to drop out with overheating troubles. He was equally unlucky to lose the Portuguese TAP Rally in the very last minutes when fog prevented the service crew from reaching their service point to provide racing tyres for the last critical stage.

It was more than unfortunate that the British Leyland merger should have come about when the team's fortunes were at the lowest ebb and the only competitive car was nearing the end of its career.

CHAPTER 13

THE RACING MINIS

When the Competitions Department was formed at Abingdon in 1954 its brief was to go racing as well as rallying. But for the early accidents involving M Gs and Austin-Healeys in the tragic Le Mans and Tourist Trophy races of 1955, that policy might well have continued. With the consequent bad publicity of B M C's cars association with these tragedies, it was agreed that Abingdon should concentrate on rallying.

The racing activities were therefore farmed out to private teams who were to operate on B M C's behalf, with their financial support, but under their own name. B M C thus had the best of both worlds for if the team was successful it could claim its share of glory but dissociate itself from any failure. Although this book is primarily concerned with the Abingdon-prepared cars the story of the Minis raced by Abingdon-supported teams forms a significant part of the Mini story.

A very early association was formed with the Cooper Car Company who since 1962 received varying degrees of financial and material sponsorship from Abingdon to represent B M C in saloon car races. That first year could not have been more successful, with John Love winning the British Championship with support from John Whitmore. The incredible Christabel Carlisle, in a Don Moore prepared car, often added not only a little glamour to the scene but often gave the menfolk a run for their money.

In 1963 the Cooper team were represented by John Whitmore, Tim Mayer and, in several races, Paddy Hopkirk. Although the Championship fell to Jack Sear's Ford Galaxie, the performance of the Cooper cars was again one of the most spectacular features of the British Saloon car scene. In Europe, Rob Slotemaker in a Downton entered car won the 1300 cc class of the European Championship.

Towards the end of that season a new Mini team made its mark – Team Broadspeed with drivers John Handley and John Fitzpatrick. Another new team appeared in 1964, run by Ken Tyrell, who had two cars to contest the European Championship. Warwick Banks was chosen to drive a 1000 cc car while Julian Vernaeve had a 1275. Coopers pinched John Fitzpatrick from Broadspeed and retained Paddy Hopkirk – their job was to contest the British Championship. Broadspeed had a roving commission, and with drivers Ralph Broad and John Handley, this team campaigned both home and overseas events. The year's racing brought good results with Warwick Banks winning the European Championship outright for the Tyrell team and John Fitzpatrick finishing runner-up and 1300 cc class winner in the British Championship.

For 1965 there was a further re-shuffling of drivers and a re-alloca-tion of responsibilities to be shared by Coopers and Broadspeed, although the latter team had considerably less support. Coopers signed John Rhodes (1300 cc class) and Warwick Banks (1000 cc class) for the British Championship. John Fitzpatrick went back to Broad-speed for a 1000 cc drive partnering John Handley in a 1275 for the European events. John Terry acted as a third team member on occasions.

Warwick Banks finished overall runner-up in the British Champion-ship (and 1000 cc class winner) with John Rhodes in third place (and 1300 cc class winner) and the season was memorable for some splendid racing against the Superspeed Anglias of Mike Young and Chris Craft. Broadspeed found the European challenge rather hard going and through lack of finance were unable to contest all of the Champ-ionship rounds. Nevertheless on the few home events when the Broadspeed cars were driven against the Cooper team, it was clear that Ralph Broad certainly had the advantage. There was therefore not a little bit of bad feeling when, for 1966, it was announced that only Coopers would gain BMC sponsorship. Ralph Broad very quickly switched to Ford leaving John Rhodes and John Handley to team up for Coopers. It was at this time that the Cooper cars were powered by Downton prepared engines rather than those provided by Eddie Maher at BMC Engines Branch. John Rhodes had a credit-able season and the year was also memorable for the performances of the Don Moore 1000 cc car in Europe driven by Paddy Hopkirk.

The Cooper team remained the same for 1967 with John Rhodes and John Handley contesting only the British events, both now running fuel-injection engines. The Superspeed Anglias of Mike Young and Chris Craft usually had the legs of the Minis but the Cooper team remained competitive by reliability. The final round decided the Championship with the honours going to the John Fitzpatrick

1900 cc Anglia from John Rhodes. Some significant intervention through this season had come from Steve Neal in a car prepared by Arden, Harry Ratcliffe in the British Vita entry and from Gordon Spice who impressed with the forceful driving of his own car.

One name, however, that always stands out above all others in Mini racing is that of John Rhodes whose arrogant style behind the wheel is a complete contrast to this charming and unassuming character. John started racing seriously in 1960 with a new Formula Junior Cooper-BMC and after many successes became the leading driver with the Midland Racing Partnership. With this team he won 15 races including the Formula Junior Championship of Ireland. John has also shown himself to be a proficient long-distance sports car driver having won the Guards 1000 mile sports car race at Brands Hatch in an MGB with John Fitzpatrick in 1965. He has also driven sports cars with distinction at Sebring, Le Mans and the Targa Florio. Success has not spoilt this popular driver who remains a great enthusiast for all levels of motor sport, however humble the rewards. Certainly he will be remembered as one who drove Minis in a style that gave pleasure to everyone while still proving that he drove them just that little bit quicker than anyone else.

Moving on to 1968, two teams received support from Abingdon for this season – Coopers who again ran in the British Championship with 1275s for John Rhodes and Steve Neal and the British Vita team, managed by Brian Gillibrand, who ran 1000 cc cars in the European series for John Handley and Alec Poole.

Despite a season-long search for more power which not even the combined brains of BMC's Eddie Maher, British Vita's Harry Ratcliffe or even Harry Weslake could resolve, the British Vita team won through on reliability if not on speed. John Handley not only won the 1000 cc category but he was also proclaimed the unofficial European Champion by gaining more points than other drivers. Coopers on the other hand had a hard season but John Rhodes nevertheless collected the 1300 cc class win. The season was again notable for the performance of Gordon Spice in the 1300 cc Equipe Arden car.

The 1968 season had seen a closer liaison between Abingdon and their associated racing teams in terms of the exchange of technical know-how and the inter-play of drivers. Under British Leyland rule, however, the 1969 programme was to bring the termination of all support to these teams.

CHAPTER 14

LEYLAND RULE

Towards the end of the 1968 season came news of the British Leyland merger and the inevitable rumours that Competitions would be amongst the first Departments to be closed down – after all Lord Stokes had very quickly done the same thing with Triumph's Competition Shop.

At a time when we at Abingdon were already committed to a vast programme for the London-to-Sydney Marathon, this was not the best of times to begin a battle for survival. After countless indecisive and time-wasting meetings, and in an atmosphere when nobody knew to whom they were responsible, I finally managed to gain some guidance for the future.

The Department was to stay but the programme of activities was to be drastically reduced to events in those countries where our winning could give the company both marketing and publicity benefits. Lord Stokes had put the emphasis on winning which was now becoming a very tall order as far as the Mini was concerned. He had also expressed a significant dislike of rallies, principally because of their cost.

A lot of head-scratching went on as to the plans for the future, for on the rallying side clearly the Mini could hope to win but a few events, and then only by reliability rather than by a straight fight against the opposition. Very reluctantly, therefore, we were forced to reduce drastically our rally programme, and our financial commitment, by terminating contracts with Timo Makinen, Rauno Aaltonen, Tony Fall and their respective co-drivers Paul Easter, Henry Liddon and Mike Wood. As Paddy Hopkirk was at that time on a two-year contract he was retained to cover our small future rallying programme, along with his new co-driver Tony Nash.

It was as sad to have to dismiss three of the best rally teams in the world as it was, two years later to say goodbye to Abingdon itself. But it costs a lot of money to retain a top rank crew, and with the prospects of little success for the future (unless British Leyland could have produced a really competitive rally model) they were, on reflection, better off to find more competitive drives with rival teams. However much you pay a driver, his true ambition must be competition success and he can only hope to stay in the top class if he has regular practice in the right events and with the right cars.

With little chance of rally successes with the Mini, with the need to trim the Department's expenditure and with the indication that there were many of the British Leyland top brass who favoured racing rather than rallying, there seemed little option but to concentrate the 1969 programme on to the race tracks. This would not only be considerably cheaper than rallying but it also meant that British Leyland could cease paying out the considerable contributions to other racing teams who in the past had represented the Company in this field.

The decision for Abingdon to go saloon car racing with the Mini may not, on reflection, have been entirely right, but then we did not deserve the continuation of the bad luck that had dogged the team in the preceding season. But I am sure, knowing the background behind that decision, there was no other alternative at the time that would have saved the Department from instant closure.

The final go ahead to the racing plan was made at a very late stage and when everyone was much more concerned with preparations for the London-to-Sydney Marathon. There was very little time to get the race cars built and properly tested before the first event at Easter. Then we had to learn a lot about fuel-injection engines which had only been used once before on a rally car. Having decided that we would build our own engines at Abingdon we then found that British Leyland had very effectively cut off the means by which we and other teams had previously been able to obtain many special parts.

To drive the cars we signed John Rhodes and John Handley while Steve Neal and Gordon Spice went to the Britax-Cooper-Downton team which had decided to carry on on its own without British Leyland's support. I had tried to persuade John Cooper to run in the 1000 cc class for the British Championship for it was clear that a competitive 1 litre Mini stood a very good chance of success. John, I know, would have liked to have done this (even with one car) but I suspect that he was influenced by his two forceful drivers, Neal and Spice, who were reluctant to drive in the small car class and were desperately keen to prove a point against the works men, Rhodes and Handley! One man who did see reason was Jim Whitehouse of Equipe Arden who prepared and entered a 1 litre car for Alec Poole who successfully pulled off the Championship.

Fated Brands opener

It was to Abingdon's credit that despite every problem the two immaculate race cars were rolled out of the transporter at the opening British Saloon Car Championship round at Brands Hatch in March. Already their performance at a Silverstone test day had shown them to be quite competitive. But the team's hard efforts were not to be rewarded.

The saloon car race was run in two heats and, in the first, John Rhodes's car was completely written off in a starting grid pile up. Then, in the closing laps of the second heat, John Handley went off the road and his car too was completely wrecked. With our shortage of cars and spare parts we were banking on getting through the first meeting unscathed to allow more development work and testing before the next event, which was only in two weeks time. To have both cars completely destroyed first time out seriously hampered our plans and the morale amongst the rally lovers could not have been lower.

But two more cars were hastily built and, untried and untested, ran at the Silverstone meeting. Although they ran well, and Rhodes and Handley were able to split the two Cooper cars, neither Mini team could get anywhere near the Broadspeed Escorts.

The Abingdon boys found it hard to adapt to the atmosphere of racing, and even harder to have to come away from a meeting without the success which they knew was expected of them. Only a few people, I was sorry to find, gave them the credit for making the switch from rallying to racing in such a desperately short time and in such difficult circumstances. It was to their credit that they proved that they could build a racing Mini to within a whisker of the incredibly high standards set by the more experienced and established teams.

Pattern of the season

Silverstone's results set the pattern for the season with the Abingdon and Cooper cars being always closely matched, neither team however being able to hold the Escorts. That Cooper often had the edge over the works cars was probably due only to the brilliance of Gordon Spice who, after a somewhat erratic past career, had suddenly found superb form.

Certainly both the Mini teams provided some of the closest racing of the season and I am sure that both lost out to the Ford opposition on many occasions because they were racing against each other and not racing together against the Escorts. In front of the pits where John Cooper and I could see what they were up to, the boys behaved themselves but I have seen some very alarming pictures of what was going on around the rest of the circuit!

This was well demonstrated in the few European events that the Abingdon cars contested, where the team faired very much better, and against some formidable 1300 cc opposition. There were worthwhile outings to the Six Hour race at the Nurburgring and to Hockenhiem while at Spa, John Handley and Roger Enever led their class all the way until the very last of the 24 hours when the car threw a rod. At least the season ended on a happy note when John Rhodes and John Handley scored a 1-2 race win at the Salzburg meeting in October.

Rallycross

The 1969 season brought the first of regular televised Rallycross events and the Abingdon team entered this new sport with a vengeance. Knowing of Lord Stokes's love of good publicity and saving the budget I reckoned that Rallycross offered the best return for money with some eight million viewers – more motor sport spectators in one afternoon than pay to watch motor racing in a whole season.

After a few early trials and tribulations, the regular team of John Rhodes and John Handley became very competitive with fuel-injection cars. We also signed up two of the leading privateers to run works cars – Brian Chatfield and Jeff Williamson. With the admirable support of these clubmen, the Rallycross Minis provided Abingdon with most of the seasons 'wins' – albeit all four 'heroes' were well and truly thrashed in the Championship honours by the unbeatable clubman, Hugh Wheldon.

Rallycross however was not only good publicity and very good fun, it also provided the team with a useful free-for-all development programme which gave us the opportunity to try out all sorts of ideas that could have been of use for future rally development.

Rallying 1969

The season's rallying programme was a mere shadow of the team's former activities and for our lone team of Paddy Hopkirk and Tony Nash it brought an endless run of 'seconds'.

On his favourite event, the Circuit of Ireland, Paddy was runner-up to Roger Clark's Escort. This was the first time that Paddy had used a limited slip differential and 12 in. wheels and, with more time for testing, this should have been a better result.

With the team's racing experience and rallying background we felt that the Mini would go well in the revived Tour de France, run in September. We entered two 1275s – a carburetter car for Paddy Hopkirk and Tony Nash and a fuel-injection one for John Handley and Paul Easter. A third Group I car was entered for Brian Culcheth and Johnstone Syer.

The new partnership of Handley and Easter worked admirably until the very last test when John went off the road when lying in a fantastic sixth place overall. Paddy moved up to take over the 1300 cc class win against considerable opposition. In the equally well-contested Group I category, Brian Culcheth had a battle royal with Julien Vernaeve's privately entered Mini, Brian finally coming off second best to the Belgian mumbling something about some cars being more standard than others! In all, the Tour was one of our more successful ventures, bringing back memories of the classic Paddy Hopkirk performance with the Mini in the 1963 event.

Another Marathon, this time the *Daily Mirror* World Cup Rally from London to Mexico, completely overshadowed all other activities at Abingdon during the latter half of 1969 and early 1970. All efforts were now centred on the development and testing of the teams of Triumph 2·5 PIs and Maxis, although one Mini Clubman was entered, by the BBC Grandstand Sports programme, for John Handley and Paul Easter.

The plan was that the Mini would be the trail blazer for the British Leyland team and John's instructions were 'to lead at Lisbon or bust'. John put in a tremendous amount of testing and, with Paul, tackled recce after recce in Europe. But that Mini entry seemed to be jinxed! Snow prevented the team from carrying out their complete recce and just about everything went wrong with the car before it reached the start line. On the event, elusive fuel starvation on the Yugoslavian stage caused problems, then the engine started to use gallons of oil and finally it blew to pieces on the Italian stage.

For John Handley that was the last of a long line of unhappy drives with the team and I have never ceased to admire the way in which this charming driver accepted the Minis failures with such good humour. John has been driving Minis in competition longer than anyone for he bought one of the very first 850s – and he can look back on a decade of Mini racing and rallying. Although he is best known for his Mini racing exploits, in his earlier days he did a lot of rallying, including three Montes, three Alpines, three Tulips and the Tour de Corse. In his later years John served as the eternal 'number two' to John Rhodes and it was a classic partnership. While Rhodes had the fire to set the pace, Handley's less forceful driving style made him the ideal man to follow through and support his team mate. That is not to say that it was always Rhodes who set the pace and Handley, on his day, and particularly in the wet, often proved unbeatable. But the ever-sincere John Handley would be the first to admit that it was not always 'his' day and certainly it was not 'his' year when he drove for Abingdon!

The final rally

To redeem faith in the Mini, Paddy Hopkirk took the World Cup Rally Clubman off to the Scottish Rally in June. Once Paddy had decided that he favoured 10 in. rather than 12 in. wheels, he and Tony Nash enjoyed a splendid rally, just failing to catch the eventual winner, Brian Culcheth in a 2·5 PI Triumph. Paddy was in tremendous form in what turned out to be his last drive for the team. Without begrudging the popular and talented Brian Culcheth his first international rally win, it would have been appropriate for Paddy to have finished with the 'win' that had eluded him so often during this last season.

Included in the racing programme for the year was the lone Group 6 Mini entry in the 86 Hours Marathon de la Route at the Nurburgring.. The car was an ultra-lightweight Clubman driven by John Handley, Alec Poole and Geoff Mabbs to back up the main Abingdon entry – the Rover 3500. Both cars led the field by an incredible margin for some 12 hours before the Mini went out with a blown head gasket and the Rover was withdrawn with a bad prop shaft vibration.

The showing of the Rover against all the works Porsches was quite sensational and the European motoring press in particular reported in glowing terms how British Leyland had demonstrated the potential of a new competition car to replace the ageing Mini. But nobody in the Abingdon team cared very much, for on the eve of the event they had been told that this trip was to be the swan song for Competitions Department.

CHAPTER 15

OBITUARY

It would be easy now for me to complete this story with bitter and biased comment about the closure of the Competitions Department, especially knowing that many people (and certainly those who have read this story so far) would join me in deploring Lord Stokes's decision. But it is not really fair to be brave and outspoken in print, especially in a book, when you know that those who share an opposite opinion do not have a chance to present their side of the argument. I will therefore present only the facts and the opinions that were expressed at the time.

Almost one month before the announcement of the closure of the Department I presented my resignation as Competitions Manager. I did so in protest against the growing frustrations of trying to get a properly planned long-term programme agreed for the future – the only plan that could have redeemed the former supremacy of the team. This I felt was essential to restore the morale of the mechanics, the loyalties of the drivers and to give the whole team some confidence and purpose for the future.

There is, in my opinion, only one way to run a Competitions Department – the way that was proved so successful in the B M C days. Well before the start of the new season, a meeting of the Competitions Committee was called, representing engineering, development, publicity and management chiefs. The Competitions Manager set out what he hoped to achieve in the coming year and the Committee members put forward their views, perhaps indicating that they would welcome publicity or development with certain models and in certain countries. A general outline of the programme was worked out, the Department received its budget and the Manager was told to achieve his objective within that budget. The Committee did not meet again until the end of the year when, if the programme had been successful, the Competitions Manager received a pat on the back and immediately asked for a bigger budget for the coming year. If it had not been a successful season then he'd got to think up some very good reasons.

There can be no future for a Competitions Department run by Committee, for too many people consider themselves experts in the field and like to lay claim to decision-making for success. But nobody stands by the Competitions Manager when he has to account for the overspending of the often futile and unsuccessful publicity 'gimmicks', foisted upon the team by the big spenders in the P R department. Time has proved that the management must put complete faith in the Competitions Manager to play the ever-changing 'chess-game' of international competitions as he sees fit in the midst of battle. There is seldom time for his decisions to be ratified by Committee.

Running the Department in this way was clearly quite unacceptable or incomprehensible to the British Leyland Management. Certainly it could not hope to conform to the whims of the finance wizards who were calling the tune in those troubled times. Above all, I always had the feeling that the management, nearly all proud Triumph men, somehow resented the reputation and prestige that the Competitions Department had brought to Abingdon and to M G, their former and always more successful rivals in the sports car market. It was in an atmosphere where every move seemed destructive rather than con- structive, critical rather than sympathetic to our problems of the time, that I decided that the time had come for me to leave Abingdon. I resigned in disagreement with future competitions policies but at least in the knowledge that a reasonable programme of events was agreed for 1971 and the budgets were signed and sealed. And the future was not all that black.

Every team has its ups and downs and, as Abingdon had proved over the last couple of years, team spirit and the will to win can pull you through even if you have not on paper got the winning car. The revival of rally development work on the Mini after the vast Triumph programme for the World Cup Rally, indicated that the Mini could still have been competitive on selected events. If as much time had been bent on Mini rough road testing as had been spent on the 1800's and Triumphs for the Marathons, it would have been a very different story. The disappointing racing season had at least taught us a lot about fuel injection engines and, with the right priorities on homologa- tion, this might well have given the Mini the added power required to be competitive in Group 2.

As for the other models in the range, we had already worked wonders with the 1800. The Maxi was coming along well and a really competitive Group 6 car was waiting for trials in the Spanish

Rally. The 2·5 PI Triumph was well-proven as an unbeatable rough-road 'tank' when speed and reliability counted. We were also working with Triumphs on what could have been a very interesting competition version of the Toledo. There was growing enthusiasm too at Rovers for the racing 3500, Abingdon inspired and financed but built and developed by Bill Shaw. This car was already the club racing saloon to beat and, in fully developed Group 2 form, it could well have been invincible on the international scene.

I felt, therefore, that there were several exciting and worthwhile prospects ahead for the Abingdon team which could well be moulded into shape with the fresh enthusiasm of a new and more politically patient leader. It was therefore as big a shock to me as it was to the others in the team to hear rumours of the complete closure of the Department. The news came through almost a month after my resignation although I was staying on at Abingdon awaiting the appointment of my successor. These rumours were finally confirmed in a meeting with Lord Stokes when our very brief talk indicated that no further discussion on the subject would change the decision.

Of the many reasons given for the closure of the Department, it seems that the saving of finance was the most logical, bearing in mind the desperate financial situation of the Company at that time. Excluding the costs of the Marathons, which were financed from separate budgets, the annual expenditure on Competitions was around £200,000. Considered as purely publicity expenditure it probably compared on average with the individual costs of other associated publicity activities such as advertising, motor shows, the press fleet, new model presentations and general publicity brochures. From British Leyland's viewpoint Competitions was the one that was the easiest to strike off the list and its rewards were probably less tangible than the rest.

But little attention, in my opinion, was given to the ever-growing profits of the Special Tuning Department who sold parts that were developed, tested, publicized and homologated by Competitions. Their annual profit was fast approaching the £100,000 mark and if the programme of expansion and improved publicity and marketing facilities had been carried out, there was little doubt that very soon the two Departments could have run as a self-financing operation. Some of the new ideas for Special Tuning have since been put into effect and with good results, but with no Competitions Department to pioneer and homologate new parts and new models I cannot foresee a profitable future. Furthermore, with no British Leyland works teams now competing and thus no works support for private entrants, there has already been a marked move, particularly amongst Europeans, to compete with other marques.

As sad as the closing of the Department was the fact that only a handful of the team were offered worthwhile jobs in other Departments. It was hoped that at least a nucleus of the old team could have been retained with Special Tuning so that their experience and knowledge could have seen the continuation of development, testing and homologation. And, if there was ever a change of heart, it would have been possible to revive a new team around this nucleus. Yet only three mechanics were retained within Special Tuning and it seemed so illogical that their less experienced staff should remain employed while the acknowledged expertise of the Competitions team was ignored and it was they who were made redundant.

At a time when there were large redundancies at M G, the management did everything possible to find jobs that would at least keep the men at Abingdon but it was nevertheless sad to see such talent wasted on menial production jobs. Doug Watts is back to his old job on rectification and road test while Tommy Wellman and Den Green are now line foremen. The only job that could be found for Cliff Humphries, the man who knows more about building and developing competition engines than most, is that of a humble supervisor on the M G trim line. The rest of the team have either left Abingdon or they have remained in the general labour pool waiting for production line jobs to come up or their time for redundancy.

There is, it seems, no place for nostalgia or sentimentality in successful big business today. Neither is there time to consider the intangible values of loyalty, enthusiasm and prestige. In its giant strides to yet further rationalization, re-organization and mergers towards survival, the men of the Competitions Department will not be the last in British Leyland to loose their jobs.

But it is more than sad that of all that British Leyland inherited from B M C, Abingdon's Competition team was one unit that did its job rather better than most. Without doubt the little red and white Minis created all over the world a record of achievement and prestige in the field of international competition that was the envy of every other manufacturer. That record book is finally closed and it is doubtful whether any other manufacturer will ever equal the achievements of the works Minis.

INTRODUCTION TO THE APPENDICES

In the following pages I have tried to document as completely as possible all of the works Mini entries in international races and rallies. I have also drawn up a table showing the competition history of each car.

It is not until one comes to compile tables such as these that one brings to light the very scanty records that were maintained by the Competitions Department and the inaccuracies which have been perpetuated by previous writers and the succession of Abingdon's Competition Press Officers (including myself) who at the time were not as diligent as we might have been in keeping the records up to date.

When it comes to quoting registration, chassis and engine numbers for the works cars, readers should bear in mind that Abingdon, like all Competitions Departments, were past masters at maintaining their legal fleet by constantly swopping engine and chassis plates. The details shown on the following tables were those that appeared on the original log book and those cars that did a lot of events were probably rebuilt with a succession of new bodies and new engines.

Inevitably there is some information missing in the following tables; I hope that there are not too many mistakes! If any reader is able to fill in any of the gaps or make any corrections I hope that they will not hesitate to pass on the information so that we may straighten the record.

APPENDIX I ABINGDON PREPARED MINI ENTRIES IN INTERNATIONAL RACES AND RALLIES

Date	Event	Driver/Co-driver	Model	Reg. No.	Comp. No.	Result	
November 1959	R A C Rally	P. Ozanne/N. Gilmour	850	TMO 559	129	Retired	
		A. Pitts/A. Ambrose	850	TMO 560	135	Retired	
		K. James,	850	TMO 561		Retired	
December 1959	Portuguese Rally	N. Mitchell/P. Allison	850	TJB 199	57	54th overall	
		P. Riley/A. Ambrose	850				
January 1960	Monte Carlo Rally	P. Riley/R. Jones	850	618 AOG	110	23rd overall	
		D. Morley/E. Morley	850	TMO 561	263	33rd overall	
		T. Wisdom/J. Hay	850	619 AOG	299	55th overall	
		A. Pitts/A. Ambrose	850	TMO 560	284	73rd overall	
		N. Mitchell/P. Allison	850	617 AOG	18	Retired	
		P. Ozanne/N. Gilmour	850	TMO 559	307	Retired	
April 1960	Geneva Rally	D. Morley/E. Morley	850	618 AOG	44	14th overall	1st class
		P. Ozanne/P. Allison	850	617 AOG	47	27th overall	2nd class
		A. Pitts/A. Ambrose	850	619 AOG	45	Crashed	
April 1960	Circuit of Ireland	D. Hiam/A. Ambrose	850	TMO 559		Retired	
May 1960	Tulip Rally	T. Christie/N. Paterson	850	TMO 560	161	36th overall	3rd class
		J. Sprinzel/M. Hughes	850	TJB 199	78	43rd overall	2nd class
		P. Ozanne/P. Allison	850	TMO 561	159	72nd overall	6th class
May 1960	Acropolis Rally	J. Milne/W. Bradley	850	619 AOG	124	15th overall	2nd class
		M. Sutcliffe/D. Astle	850	618 AOG	122	31st overall	5th class
		P. Ozanne/P. Allison	850	617 AOG	120	Retired	
June 1960	Alpine Rally	T. Gold/M. Hughes	850	TMO 561	19	14th overall	1st class
		A. Pitts/A. Ambrose	850	TMO 560	1		4th class
		K. James/R. Jones	850	TMO 559	5	Crashed	
November 1960	R A C Rally	D. Seigle-Morris/V. Elford	850	TMO 559	183	6th overall	2nd class
		M. Sutcliffe/D. Astle	850	TMO 561	170	8th overall	4th class
		T. Christie/N. Paterson	850	TMO 560	174	Retired	

172

Date	Rally	Crew	Car	No.	Result	Class
January 1961	Monte Carlo Rally	P. Garnier/R. Jones	850 TMO 559	254	Retired	
		T. Christie/N. Paterson	850 TMO 560	227	Retired	
		D. Astle/S. Woolley	850 TMO 561	226	Retired	
March 1961	Lyon–Charbonnières Rally	P. Moss/A. Wisdom	850 TMO 560		Retired	
May 1961	Tulip Rally	P. Riley/A. Ambrose	850 TMO 561	136	12th overall	1st class
		D. Seigle-Morris/V. Elford	850 TMO 559		23rd overall	3rd class
May 1961	Acropolis Rally	M. Sutcliffe/D. Astle	850 619 AOG	115	Retired	
		D. Seigle-Morris/V. Elford	850 TMO 560		Crashed	
		D. Morley/A. Wisdom	850 363 DOC		Crashed	
January 1962	Monte Carlo Rally	P. Moss/A. Wisdom	997 737 ABL	304	26th overall	7th class Coupe des Dames
		R. Jones/P. Morgan	850 363 DOC	97	77th overall	3rd class
		R. Aaltonen/G. Mabbs	997		Crashed	
May 1962	Tulip Rally	P. Moss/A. Wisdom	997 737 ABL	104	1st overall	1st class Coupe des Dames
		D. Seigle-Morris/A. Ambrose	850 363 DOC		Retired	
June 1962	Alpine Rally	R. Aaltonen/G. Palm	997 407 ARX	63	Retired	
August 1962	1000 Lakes Rally	R. Aaltonen/A. Ambrose	997 407 ARX		Retired	
September 1962	Baden-Baden Rally	P. Moss/P. Mayman	997 737 ABL		1st overall	1st class Coupe des Dames
October 1962	Geneva Rally	P. Moss/P. Mayman	997 737 ABL	135	3rd overall	1st class
November 1962	R A C Rally	R. Aaltonen/A. Ambrose	997 977 ARX	6	5th overall	1st class
		T. Makinen/J. Steadman	997 407 ARX	38	7th overall	1st class
		L. Morrison/R. Finlay	997 477 ABL	32	13th overall	3rd class

Date	Event	Driver/Co-driver	Model	Reg. No.	Comp. No.	Result	Class
January 1963	Monte Carlo Rally	R. Aaltonen/A. Ambrose	997	977 ARX	288	3rd overall	1st class
		P. Hopkirk/J. Scott	997	407 ARX	66	6th overall	2nd class
		P. Mayman/V. Domleo	997	737 ABL		28th overall	
		L. Morrison/B. Culcheth	997	477 ABL	155	44th overall	1st class
April 1963	Tulip Rally	P. Hopkirk/H. Liddon	997	17 CRX	130	2nd overall	1st class
		P. Mayman/V. Domleo	997	737 ABL	129	21st overall	4th class
May 1963	Trifels Rally	P. Mayman/V. Domleo	997	737 ABL			1st class / Coupe des Dames
June 1963	Scottish Rally	L. Morrison/D. Brown	997			Crashed	
June 1963	Alpine Rally	R. Aaltonen/A. Ambrose	1071	277 EBL	63	1st overall	1st class / Coupe des Alpes
		P. Mayman/V. Domleo	997	18 CRX	73	6th overall	1st class / Coupe des Alpes / Coupe des Dames
		J. Sprinzel/W. Cave	997	977 ARX	24	Crashed	
		D. McCluggage/R. Seers	997	17 CRX	64	Retired	
September 1963	Tour de France	P. Hopkirk/H. Liddon	1071	33 EJB	38	3rd overall	1st class
		R. Aaltonen/A. Ambrose	1071	477 ABL	24	44th overall	
		T. Makinen/L. Morrison	1071	407 ARX	27	Retired	
		P. Mayman/E. Jones	1071	277 EBL	39	Retired	

Date / Rally	Crew	Car	No.	Result	Class
November 1963 R A C Rally	P. Hopkirk/H. Liddon	1071 8 EMO	21	4th overall	2nd touring class
	L. Morrison/R. Finlay	970 407 ARX	36	19th overall	1st class
	P. Mayman/V. Domleo	1071 277 EBL	38	30th overall	
January 1964 Monte Carlo Rally	P. Hopkirk/H. Liddon	1071 33 EJB	37	1st overall	1st class
	T. Makinen/P. Vanson	1071 570 FMO	182	4th overall	2nd class
	R. Aaltonen/A. Ambrose	1071 569 FMO	105	7th overall	3rd class
	R. Baxter/E. McMillan	997 477 ABL	39	43rd overall	2nd class
	P. Mayman/V. Domleo	1071 277 EBL	189	Crashed	
	J. Thompson/F. Heys	1071 18 CRX	187	Crashed	
				(Manufacturers Team Prize)	
April 1964 Tulip Rally	T. Makinen/A. Ambrose	1275 AJB 66B	119	1st overall	1st class
				(Manufacturers Team Prize with P. Riley and J. Vernaeve)	
May 1964 Acropolis Rally	P. Hopkirk/H. Liddon	1275 AJB 55B	67	Retired	
	R. Aaltonen/A. Ambrose	1275 AJB 33B		Retired	
June 1964 Alpine Rally	R. Aaltonen/A. Ambrose	1275 AJB 55B	70	4th category	1st class Coupe des Alpes
	P. Mayman/V. Domleo	997 AJB 66B	8	6th category	1st class Coupe des Dames
	P. Hopkirk/H. Liddon	1275 AJB 44B	18	Retired	
	T. Makinen/P. Vanson	1275 BJB 77B	19	Retired	
				(Manufacturers Team Prize)	

175

Date	Event	Driver/Co-driver	Model	Reg. No.	Comp. No.	Result
August 1964	1000 Lakes Rally	T. Makinen/P. Keskitalo	1275	AJB 33B	68	4th overall, 1st class
August 1964	Spa–Sofia–Liège Rally	J. Wadsworth/M. Wood	1275	570 FMO		20th overall
September 1964	Tour de France	P. Mayman/V. Domleo	970	AJB 66B	20	1st class
		P. Hopkirk/H. Liddon	970	AJB 44B	19	Retired
		R. Aaltonen/A. Ambrose	1275	AJB 55B	30	Retired
		T. Makinen/P. Easter	970	BJB 77B	18	Crashed
November 1964	R A C Rally	P. Hopkirk/H. Liddon	1275	CRX 90B	1	Retired
		R. Aaltonen/A. Ambrose	1275	CRX 89B	2	Retired
		C. Orrenius/R. Dahlgren	1275	AJB 44B	37	Retired
		H. Kallstrom/R. Haakansson	1275	AGU 780B	42	Retired
January 1965	Monte Carlo Rally	T. Makinen/P. Easter	1275	AJB 44B	52	1st overall, 1st class
		P. Hopkirk/H. Liddon	1275	CRX 91B	56	26th overall, 1st class
		D. Morley/E. Morley	1275	CRX 90B	72	27th overall, 2nd class
		R. Aaltonen/A. Ambrose	1275	CRX 88B	273	Retired
		H. Kallstrom/R. Haakansson	1275	AGU 780B	176	Retired
		R. Baxter/J. Scott	1275	8 EMO	91	Retired
February 1965	Swedish Rally	P. Hopkirk/H. Liddon	1275	AJB 33B	28	Retired
		R. Aaltonen/A. Ambrose	1275	DJB 93B	22	Retired
		T. Makinen/P. Easter	1275	DJB 92B	31	Retired
		H. Kallstrom/R. Haakansson	1275	AGU 780B		Retired
March 1965	Circuit of Ireland	P. Hopkirk/T. Harryman	1275	CRX 89B	2	1st overall, 1st class
April 1965	Tulip Rally	T. Makinen/P. Easter	1275	AJB 33B	124	3rd category, 1st class
May 1965	Acropolis Rally	T. Makinen/P. Easter	1275	DJB 93B	60	Retired
June 1965	Scottish Rally	P. Hopkirk/H. Liddon	1275	CRX 89B	3	Retired

Date	Rally	Crew		Car	No.	Overall	Class
June 1965	Geneva Rally	R. Aaltonen/A. Ambrose		EBL 55C	64	1st overall	1st class
July 1965	Czech Rally	R. Aaltonen/A. Ambrose	1275	EJB 55C	102	1st overall	1st class
		T. Makinen/P. Easter	1275	AJB 66B	100	Retired	
July 1965	Nordrhein–Wesfalen Rally	P. Hopkirk/H. Liddon	1275	DJB 92B	58	6th overall	1st class
July 1965	Alpine Rally	T. Makinen/P. Easter	1275	AJB 33B	70	2nd touring category	1st touring class, Coupe des Alpes
		P. Hopkirk/H. Liddon	1275	EBL 56C	60	4th category	2nd class, Coupe des Alpes
		R. Aaltonen/A. Ambrose	1275	EBL 55C	56	14th overall	13th category
		P. Mayman/V. Domleo	1275	DJB 93B	66	Coupe des Dames	(Manufacturers Team Prize)
July 1965	Polish Rally	R. Aaltonen/A. Ambrose	1275	CRX 89B	55	1st overall	1st touring class
August 1965	1000 Lakes Rally	T. Makinen/P. Keskitalo	1275	AJB 33B	28	1st overall	1st class
		R. Aaltonen/A. Jaervi	1275	EBL 55C	22	2nd overall	2nd class
		P. Hopkirk/K. Ruutsalo	1275	EBL 56C		6th overall	
						(Manufacturers Team Prize)	
October 1965	Munich–Vienna–Budapest Rally	R. Aaltonen/A. Ambrose	1275	CRX 89B	72	1st overall	1st class
		A. Fall/R. Crellin	1275	AJB 55B	65	Crashed	2nd class
		G. Halliwell/M. Wood	1275	CRX 90B		(Manufacturers Team Prize)	

177

Date	Event	Driver/Co-driver	Model	Reg. No.	Comp. No.	Result	
November 1965	R A C Rally	R. Aaltonen/A. Ambrose	1275	DJB 93B	5	1st overall	1st class
		J. Lusenius/M. Wood	1275	DJB 92B	44	6th overall	1st class
		P. Hopkirk/H. Liddon	1275	EBL 56C	8	13th overall	2nd class
		A. Fall/R. Crellin	1275	CRX 89B	36	15th overall	3rd class
		H. Kallstrom/N. Bjork	1275	EJB 55C	37	Retired	
January 1966	Monte Carlo Rally	T. Makinen/P. Easter	1275	GRX 55D	2	Disqualified	
		R. Aaltonen/A. Ambrose	1275	GRX 55D	242	Disqualified	
		P. Hopkirk/H. Liddon	1275	GRX 5D	230	Disqualified	
		R. Baxter/J. Scott	1275	GRX 195D	87	Disqualified	
February 1966	Swedish Rally	R. Aaltonen/H. Liddon	1275	GRX 310D	35	Retired	
		T. Makinen/P. Easter	1275	DJB 92B		Retired	
February 1966	Rally of the Flowers	P. Hopkirk/R. Crellin	1275	GRX 309D	50	15th overall	6th touring class
		A. Fall/H. Liddon	1275	GRX 5D		Disqualified	
April 1966	Circuit of Ireland	A. Fall/H. Liddon	1275	DJB 92B	4	1st overall	1st touring class
		P. Hopkirk/T. Harryman	1275	GRX 55D	1	Crashed	
April 1966	Tulip Rally	R. Aaltonen/H. Liddon	1275	GRX 310D	89	1st overall	1st class
		T. Makinen/P. Easter	1275	GRX 5D	100	9th overall (Manufacturers Team Prize with R. Freeborough)	1st class
May 1966	Austrian Alpine Rally	P. Hopkirk/R. Crellin	1275	DJB 92B	58	1st overall	1st class
		A. Fall/M. Wood	1275	GRX 310D		Retired	

Date	Rally	Drivers		Car	No.	Position	Class
May 1966	Acropolis Rally	P. Hopkirk/R. Crellin	1275	GRX 311D	67	3rd overall	1st touring class
		T. Makinen/P. Easter	1275	HJB 656D	82	10th overall	2nd touring class
		R. Aaltonen/H. Liddon	1275	JBL 172D	77	Retired	
June 1966	Scottish Rally	A. Fall/M. Wood	1275	DJB 93B		1st overall	1st touring class
June 1966	Geneva Rally	A. Fall/H. Liddon	1275	EBL 56C	75	2nd overall	2nd touring class
		P. Hopkirk/T. Harryman	1275	JBL 495D	50	Retired	
		(Manufacturers Team Prize with G. Theiler and D. Friswell)					
June 1966	London Rally	P. Hopkirk/R. Crellin	1275	JBL 495D	6	Retired	
		A. Fall/M. Wood	1275	DJB 93B	4	Retired	
July 1966	Czech Rally	R. Aaltonen/H. Liddon	1275	JBL 494D	75	1st overall	1st class
		T. Makinen/P. Easter	1275	JBL 493D	77	3rd overall	2nd class
		S. Zasada/Z. Leszczuk	1275	EBL 56C	16	4th overall	1st class
						(Manufacturers Team Prize)	
July 1966	German Rally	P. Hopkirk/C. Nash	1275	GRX 311D	42	Retired	
		A. Fall/H. Liddon	1275	JBL 172D	49	Retired	
August 1966	Polish Rally	A. Fall/A. Krauklis	970	GRX 309D	56	1st overall	1st class
		T. Makinen/P. Easter	1275	HJB 656D	28	2nd overall	1st class
		R. Aaltonen/H. Liddon	1275	GRX 555D	37	Retired	
August 1966	Welsh Rally	A. Fall/M. Wood	1275	GRX 309D		Retired	

Date	Event	Driver/Co-driver	Model	Reg. No.	Comp. No.	Result	
August 1966	1000 Lakes Rally	T. Makinen/P. Keskitalo	1275	JBL 493D	45	1st overall	1st class
		R. Aaltonen/V. Numimaa	1275	GRX 310D	49	3rd overall	2nd class
		J. Lusenius/K. Lehto	1275	JBL 494D		6th overall	3rd class
September 1966	Alpine Rally	R. Aaltonen/H. Liddon	1275	JBL 495D	62	3rd overall	2nd class
		P. Hopkirk/R. Crellin	1275	GRX 311D		Retired	
		T. Makinen/P. Easter	1275	JMO 969D	68	Retired	
		A. Fall/M. Wood	1275	GRX 195D	66	Retired	
October 1966	Munich–Vienna–Budapest Rally	T. Makinen/P. Easter	1275	HJB 656D	57	1st overall	1st class
		A. Fall/H. Liddon	1275	JBL 494D		Retired	
November 1966	R A C Rally	H. Kallstrom/R. Haakansson	1275	JBL 494D	66	2nd overall	1st class
		R. Aaltonen/H. Liddon	1275	GRX 310D	18	4th overall	2nd class
		A. Fall/M. Wood	1275	GRX 195D	21	5th overall	3rd class
		M. Aaltonen/C. Tyler	1275	EBL 56C	117	37th overall	
		P. Hopkirk/R. Crellin	1275	JMO 969D	10	Retired	
		T. Makinen/P. Easter	1275	GRX 5D	12	Retired	
		S. Lampinen/A. Ambrose	1275	JBL 495D	29	Crashed	
		G. Hill/M. Boyd	1275	GRX 309D	5	Retired	
January 1967	Monte Carlo Rally	R. Aaltonen/H. Liddon	1275	LBL 6D	177	1st overall	1st class
		P. Hopkirk/R. Crellin	1275	LBL 666D	205	6th overall	5th class
		A. Fall/R. Joss	1275	LBL 606D	32	10th overall	
		S. Lampinen/M. Wood	1275	HJB 656D	178	15th overall	
		T. Makinen/P. Easter	1275	LBL 66D	144	41st overall	
February 1967	Swedish Rally	R. Aaltonen/H. Liddon	1275	JBL 495D	26	3rd overall	1st class
		T. Makinen/P. Easter	1275	JMO 969D	22	Retired	
February 1967	Rally of the Flowers	P. Hopkirk/R. Crellin	1275	LBL 590E	67	2nd overall	2nd class
		A. Fall/M. Wood	1275	GRX 195D	82	4th overall	4th class
March 1967	East African Safari	R. Aaltonen/H. Liddon	1275	HJB 656D	8	Retired	
March 1967	Circuit of Ireland	P. Hopkirk/T. Harryman	1275	GRX 5D	1	1st overall	1st class
March 1967	Sebring 3 Hour Race	P. Hopkirk/J. Rhodes	1275	GRX 309D	48	1st overall	1st class
April 1967	Tulip Rally	T. Makinen/P. Easter	1275	LRX 827E	64	2nd overall	1st category
		R. Aaltonen/H. Liddon	1275	LRX 829E	65	3rd overall	2nd category
		D. Benzimra/T. Harryman	1275	GRX 5D	73	Retired	

(Manufacturers Team Prize with J. Vernaeve)

Date	Rally	Drivers		Reg.	No.	Result	Class
May 1967	Acropolis Rally	P. Hopkirk/R. Crellin	1275	LRX 830E	89	1st overall	1st class
		R. Aaltonen/H. Liddon	1275	LRX 828E	92	Retired	
		T. Makinen/P. Easter	1275	GRX 195D	99	Retired	
June 1967	Scottish Rally	L. Ytterbring/L. Persson	1275	GRX 311D	1	2nd overall	
		A. Fall/M. Wood	1275	GRX 5D		Retired	
June 1967	Geneva Rally	A. Fall/M. Wood	1275	LRX 829E	79	1st overall	1st class
		J. Vernaeve/H. Liddon	1275	LRX 827E	80	2nd overall	2nd class
July 1967	London Rally	A. Fall/M. Wood	1275	GRX 5D	8	Retired	
July 1967	Danube Rally	R. Aaltonen/H. Liddon	1275	LRX 828E		Disqualified	
August 1967	1000 Lakes Rally	T. Makinen/P. Keskitalo	1275	GRX 195D	29	1st overall	1st class
August 1967	Marathon de la Route	A. Fall/J. Vernaeve/A. Hedges	970	GRX 5D	39	2nd overall	
		A. Poole/R. Enever/C. Baker	970	LRX 830E	40	Retired	
September 1967	Alpine Rally	P. Hopkirk/R. Crellin	1275	LRX 827E	107	1st overall	1st class
		R. Aaltonen/H. Liddon	1275	JBL 172D	106	Retired	
		T. Makinen/P. Easter	1275	GRX 311D	103	Retired	
		A. Fall/M. Wood	1275	GRX 310D	40	Retired	
November 1967	Tour de Corse	P. Hopkirk/R. Crellin	1275	GRX 5D	79	Retired	
		R. Aaltonen/H. Liddon	1275	JBL 172D	73	Retired	
January 1968	Monte Carlo Rally	R. Aaltonen/H. Liddon	1275	ORX 7F	18	3rd overall	1st category
		A. Fall/M. Wood	1275	ORX 707F	185	4th overall	2nd category
		P. Hopkirk/R. Crellin	1275	ORX 777F	87	5th overall	3rd category
		T. Makinen/P. Easter	1275	ORX 77F	7	55th overall (Manufacturers Team Prize)	
February 1968	Rally of the Flowers	R. Aaltonen/H. Liddon	1275	ORX 77F	40	Retired	
		A. Fall/M. Wood	1275	ORX 777F	40	Retired	
April 1968	Tulip Rally	J. Vernaeve/M. Wood	1275	ORX 707F	74	3rd overall	1st category
		T. Makinen/P. Easter	1275	LBL 66D	73	41st overall	

Date	Event	Driver/Co-driver	Model	Reg. No.	Comp. No.	Result	
April 1968	Circuit of Ireland	P. Hopkirk/T. Harryman L. Ytterbring/L. Persson	1275 1275	JMO 969D OBL 46F	1 3	Retired Retired	
April 1968	Canadian Shell 4000 Rally	P. Hopkirk/M. Kerry	1275	GRX 5D	119	Retired	
May 1968	Acropolis Rally	R. Aaltonen/H. Liddon T. Makinen/P. Easter	1275 1275	RBL 450F GRX 310D	46 49	5th overall Retired	1st class
June 1968	Scottish Rally	L. Ytterbring/L. Persson	1275	JMO 969D	3	2nd overall	1st class
October 1968	Portuguese T A P Rally	P. Hopkirk/A. Nash	1275	LBL 606D	71	2nd overall	1st class
March 1969	Brands Hatch	J. Rhodes J. Handley	1275 1275	OBL 46F OBL 45F		Crashed Crashed	
March 1969	Silverstone, Daily Express Trophy	J. Handley J. Rhodes	1275 1275	LRX 827E GRX 310D	15 14	10th overall 11th overall	4th class 5th class
April 1969	Thruxton	J. Handley J. Rhodes	1275 1275	LRX 827E GRX 310D		9th overall 22nd overall	
April 1969	Circuit of Ireland	P. Hopkirk/A. Nash	1275	GRX 311D	2	2nd overall	1st class
May 1969	Silverstone, Martini International	J. Rhodes J. Handley	1275 1275	LBL 666D LRX 827E	17 16	6th overall 7th overall	2nd class 4th class
May 1969	Crystal Palace, Anerley Trophy	J. Handley J. Rhodes	1275 1275	LRX 827E LBL 666D	135 134	3rd overall 4th overall	3rd class 4th class
June 1969	Hockenheim	J. Rhodes J. Handley	1275 1275	URX 560G URX 550G		6th overall	3rd class 5th class
June 1969	Brands Hatch Six Hours	J. Handley/R. Enever J. Rhodes/P. Hopkirk	1275 1275	RBL 450F GRX 310D		4th overall 7th overall	2nd class 3rd class
June 1969	Mallory Park, Guards International	J. Rhodes J. Handley	1275 1275	LBL 666D LRX 827E	118	8th overall 10th overall	4th class

Date	Event	Drivers		Reg.	No.	Overall	Class
July 1969	Nurburgring Six Hours	J. Handley/R. Enever	1275	RBL 450F		Retired	4th class
		J. Rhodes/G. Mabbs	1275	GRX 310D		Retired	6th class
July 1969	Silverstone, British Grand Prix	J. Rhodes	1275	LBL 666D	16	8th overall	4th class
		J. Handley	1275	LRX 827E	15	10th overall	6th class
September 1969	Spa 24 Hours	J. Handley/R. Enever	1275	RBL 450F		Retired	
September 1969	Tour de France	P. Hopkirk/A. Nash	1275	OBL 45F	57	14th overall	1st class
		J. Handley/P. Easter	1275	URX 550G	12	Crashed	
		B. Culcheth/J. Syer	1275	URX 560G	56		2nd class
August 1969	Oulton Park	J. Rhodes	1275	LBL 666D		12th overall	4th class
		J. Handley	1275	RJB 327F		15th overall	
September 1969	Brands Hatch, Guards Trophy	J. Rhodes	1275	LBL 666D	244	11th overall	4th class
		J. Handley	1275	LRX 827E	245	Retired	
October 1969	Salzburg	J. Rhodes	1275	LBL 666D		1st overall	1st class
		J. Handley	1275	LRX 827E		2nd overall	2nd class
April 1970	World Cup Rally	J. Handley/P. Easter	1275	XJB 308H	56	Retired	
June 1970	Scottish Rally	P. Hopkirk/A. Nash	1275	XJB 308H	14	2nd overall	1st class
September 1970	Marathon de la Route	J. Handley/A. Poole/J. Vernaeve	1275	SOH 878H		Retired	
October 1970	Southern Cross Rally	A. Cowan/R. Forsyth	1275	YMO 881H		Retired	
		B. Culcheth/R. Bonhomme	1275	RJB 327F		Retired	

APPENDIX II—THE WORKS MINIS

Registration number	Registered	Chassis No. Engine No.	Events	Driver	Result
TJB 199	August 1959	M/A2S4-675 8MB-U-H.899	1959 Portuguese 1960 Tulip Sold to A. Hutcheson	Mitchell Sprinzel	54th 43rd
TMO 559	October 1959	M/A2S4 4258 8MB-U-H.2890	1959 R A C 1960 Monte 1960 Circuit of Ireland 1960 Alpine 1960 R A C 1961 Monte Carlo 1961 Tulip Sold to V. Elford	Ozanne Ozanne Hiam James Seigle-Morris Garnier Seigle-Morris	Retired Retired Retired Crashed 6th Retired 23rd
TMO560	October 1959	M/A2S4 1640 8MB-U-H 2886	1959 R A C 1960 Monte Carlo 1960 Tulip 1960 Alpine 1960 R A C 1961 Monte 1961 Lyon Charbonnieres 1961 Acropolis Sold to A. Pitts	Pitts Pitts Christie Pitts Christie Christie Moss Seigle-Morris	Retired 73rd 36th 4th class Retired Retired Retired Crashed
TMO 561	October 1959	M/A2S4 4336 8MB-U-H 2495	1959 R A C 1960 Monte Carlo 1960 Tulip 1960 Alpine 1960 R A C 1961 Monte Carlo 1961 Tulip Sold to A. Wisdon	James Morley Ozanne Gold Sutcliffe Astle Riley	Retired 33rd 72nd 14th 8th Retired 12th

Reg.	Date	Numbers	Event	Driver	Result
617 AOG	November 1959	A/A2S7 7024 8A–U–H 6487	1960 Monte Carlo 1960 Geneva 1960 Acropolis Sold to P. Ozanne	Mitchell Ozanne Ozanne	Retired 27th Retired
618 AOG	November 1959	A/A2S7 7045 8A–U–H 6603	1960 Monte Carlo 1960 Geneva 1960 Acropolis Sold to M. Sutcliffe	Riley Morley Sutcliffe	23rd 14th 31st
619 AOG	November 1959	A/A2S7 7046 8A–U–H 6492	1960 Monte Carlo 1960 Geneva 1960 Acropolis 1961 Acropolis Sold to A. Farrar	Wisdom Pitts Milne Sutcliffe	55th Crashed 15th Retired
363 DOC	March 1961	A/A2S7 97971A 8AM–U–H 136551	1961 Acropolis 1962 Monte Carlo 1962 Tulip	Morley Jones Seigle-Morris	Crashed 77th Retired
737 ABL	November 1961	K.A2S7.165317 9F.SA.H 657	1962 Monte Carlo 1962 Tulip 1962 Baden–Baden 1962 Geneva 1963 Monte Carlo 1963 Tulip 1963 Trifels Sold to P. Anton	Moss Moss Moss Moss Mayman Mayman Mayman	26th 1st 1st 3rd 28th 21st 1st class
407 ARX	March 1962	K.A2S4.222450 9F.SA.H 4203	1962 Alpine 1962 1000 Lakes 1962 R A C 1963 Monte Carlo 1963 Tour de France 1963 R A C Sold to P. Riley	Aaltonen Aaltonen Makinen Hopkirk Makinen Morrison	Retired Retired 7th 6th Retired 19th

Registration number	Registered	Chassis no. Engine no.	Events	Driver	Result
977 ARX	March 1962	K.A2S4.226727 9F.SA.H 4582	1962 R A C 1963 Monte Carlo 1963 Alpine Written off	Aaltonen Aaltonen Sprinzel	5th 3rd Crashed
477 ABL	April 1962	K.A2S4 221347 9F.SA.H 4432	1962 R A C 1963 Monte Carlo 1963 Tour de France 1964 Monte Carlo Sold to M. Wood	Morrison Morrison Aaltonen Baxter	13th 44th 44th 43rd
17 CRX	December 1962	K.A2S4 318992 9F.SA.H 14732	1963 Tulip 1963 Alpine Sold to S. Turner	Hopkirk McCluggage	2nd Retired
18 CRX	December 1962	K.A2S4 318088 9F.SA.H 15276	1963 Alpine 1964 Monte Carlo Sold to P. Easter	Mayman Thompson	5th Retired
8 EMO	May 1963	K.A2S4 384848 9F.SA.Y 35510	1963 R A C 1965 Monte Carlo Sold to Oswald Tillotson Ltd.	Hopkirk Baxter	4th Retired
277 EBL	May 1963	K.A2S4 384611 9F.SA.H 19243	1963 Tour de France 1963 R A C 1964 Monte Carlo Written off	Aaltonen Mayman Mayman Mayman	1st Retired 30th Crashed
33 EJB	May 1963	K.A2S4 384627 9F.SA.H 19269	1963 Tour de France 1964 Monte Carlo Retained as display car	Hopkirk Hopkirk	3rd 1st

186

Registration	Date	Chassis / Engine No.	Events	Driver	Result
569 FMO	November 1963	C.A2S7 482488 9F.SA.H 26586	1964 Monte Carlo Sold to M. Wood	Aaltonen	7th
570 FMO	November 1963	C.A2S7 482499 9F.SA.H 26606	1964 Monte Carlo 1964 Spa–Sofia–Liège Sold to K. James	Makinen Wadsworth	4th 20th
AJB 33B	February 1964	C.A2S7 487712 9F.SA.Y 38155	1964 Acropolis 1964 1000 Lakes 1965 Swedish 1965 Tulip 1965 Alpine 1965 1000 Lakes Sold to T. Makinen	Aaltonen Makinen Hopkirk Makinen Makinen Makinen	Retired 4th Retired 3rd 2nd 1st
AJB 44B	February 1964	K.A2S4 488512 9F.SA.Y 31851	1964 Alpine 1964 Tour de France 1964 R A C 1965 Monte Carlo Retained as display car	Hopkirk Hopkirk Orrenius Makinen	Retired Retired Retired 1st
AJB 55B	February 1964	C.A2S7 487640 9F.SA.Y 31399	1964 Acropolis 1964 Alpine 1964 Tour de France 1965 Munich–Vienna–Budapest Sold to R. Haakansson	Hopkirk Aaltonen Aaltonen Fall	Retired 4th Retired 2nd class
AJB 66B	February 1964	K.A2S4 488503 9F.SA.Y 31360	1964 Tulip 1964 Alpine 1964 Tour de France 1965 Nordrhein–Westfalen Sold to J. Cracknell	Makinen Mayman Mayman Hopkirk	1st 6th 1st class Retired

Registration number	Registered	Chassis no. Engine no.	Events	Driver	Result
BJB 77B	June 1964	K.A2S4 489078 9F.SA.Y 31360	1964 Alpine 1964 Tour de France Written off	Makinen Makinen	Retired Crashed
CRX 88B	October 1964	C.A2S7 552400 9F.SA.Y 32170	1965 Monte Carlo Written off	Aaltonen	Retired
CRX 89B	October 1964	C.A2S7 552318 9F.SA.Y 32562	1964 RAC 1965 Circuit of Ireland 1965 Scottish 1965 Polish 1965 Munich–Vienna–Budapest 1965 RAC Sold to G. Mabbs	Aaltonen Hopkirk Hopkirk Aaltonen Aaltonen Fall	Retired 1st Retired 1st 1st 15th
CRX 90B	October 1964	K.A2S4 552445 9F.SA.Y 32706	1964 RAC 1965 Monte Carlo 1965 Munich–Vienna–Budapest Sold to P. Easter	Hopkirk Morley Halliwell	Retired 27th Crashed
CRX 91B	October 1964	K.A2S4 552446 9F.SA.Y 32341	1965 Monte Carlo Sold to R. Aaltonen	Hopkirk	26th
AGU 780B	November 1964	C.A25L 551892 9F.SA.Y 31798	1964 RAC 1965 Monte Carlo 1965 Swedish Sold to H. Kallstrom	Kallstrom Kallstrom Kallstrom	Retired Retired Retired
DJB 92B	December 1964	K.A2S4 553382 9F.SA.Y 34628	1965 Swedish 1965 Nordrhein–Westfalen 1965 RAC 1966 Swedish 1966 Circuit of Ireland 1966 Austrian Alpine Sold to J. Sprinzel	Makinen Hopkirk Lusenius Makinen Fall Hopkirk	Retired 6th 6th Retired 1st 1st

Reg.	Date	Chassis No.	Event	Driver	Result
DJB 93B	December 1964	C.A2S7 662044 9F.SA.Y 34709	1965 Swedish	Aaltonen	Retired
			1965 Acropolis	Makinen	Retired
			1965 Alpine	Mayman	13th
			1965 RAC	Aaltonen	1st
			1966 Scottish	Fall	1st
			1966 London	Fall	Retired
			Written off		
EJB 55C	March 1965	C.A2S7 675795 9F. SA.Y 35826	1965 Geneva	Aaltonen	1st
			1965 Czech	Aaltonen	1st
			1965 RAC	Kallstrom	Retired
			Written off		
EBL 55C	March 1965	K.A2S4 675665 9F.SA.Y 35595	1965 Alpine	Aaltonen	14th
			1965 1000 Lakes	Aaltonen	2nd
			Sold to Voimavanu, Finland		
EBL 56C	March 1965	K.A2S4 676062 9F.SA.Y 35953	1965 Alpine	Hopkirk	4th
			1965 1000 Lakes	Hopkirk	6th
			1965 RAC	Hopkirk	13th
			1966 Geneva	Fall	2nd
			1966 Czech	Zasada	4th
			1966 RAC	Aaltonen	37th
			Sold to British Vita		
GRX 5D	January 1966	C.A2S7 820483 9F.SA.Y 39689	1966 Monte Carlo	Hopkirk	Disqualified
			1966 Rally of the Flowers	Fall	Disqualified
			1966 Tulip	Makinen	9th
			1966 RAC	Makinen	Retired
			1967 Circuit of Ireland	Hopkirk	1st
			1967 Tulip	Benzinra	Retired
			1967 Scottish	Fall	Retired
			1967 London	Fall	Retired
			1967 84 Hour Marathon	Fall/Vernaeve/Hedges	2nd
			1967 Tour de Corse	Hopkirk	Retired
			1968 Shell 4000	Hopkirk	Retired
			Sold to Pressed Steel Apprentices		

Registration number	Registered	Chassis no. Engine no.	Events	Driver	Result
GRX 55D	January 1966	C.A2S7 820482 9F.SA.Y 39688	1966 Monte Carlo 1966 Circuit of Ireland Written off	Aaltonen Hopkirk	Disqualified Crashed
GRX 195D	January 1966	K.A2S4 799887 9F.SA.Y 39495	1966 Monte Carlo 1966 Alpine 1966 RAC 1967 Rally of the Flowers 1967 Acropolis 1967 1000 Lakes Sold to B. Martyn	Baxter Fall Fall Fall Makinen Makinen	Disqualified Retired 5th 4th Retired 1st
GRX 309D	January 1966	C.A2S7 799782 9F.SA.Y 39462	1966 Rally of the Flowers 1966 Polish 1966 Welsh 1966 RAC 1966 Sebring 3 Hours Race Sold to BMC USA	Hopkirk Fall Fall Hill Hopkirk/Rhodes	16th 1st Retired Retired 1st class
GRX 310D	January 1966	K.A2S4 799883	1966 Swedish 1966 Tulip 1966 Austrian Alpine 1966 1000 Lakes 1966 RAC 1967 Alpine 1968 Acropolis 1969 Silverstone 1969 Snetterton 1969 Thruxton 1969 Brands 1969 Nurburgring Sold to W. Price	Aaltonen Aaltonen Fall Aaltonen Aaltonen Fall Makinen Rhodes Rhodes Rhodes Rhodes/Hopkirk Rhodes/Mabbs	Retired 1st Retired 3rd 4th Retired Retired 11th 12th 22nd 7th Retired
GRX 555D	January 1966	K.A2S7 820484 9F.SA.Y 39690	1966 Monte Carlo 1966 Polish Sold to L. Lambourne	Makinen Aaltonen	Disqualified Retired

Reg.	Date	Numbers	Event	Driver	Result
GRX 311D	February 1966	K.A2S4 820360 9F.SA.Y 39837	1966 Acropolis	Hopkirk	3rd
			1966 German	Hopkirk	1st
			1966 Alpine	Hopkirk	Retired
			1967 Scottish	Ytterbring	2nd
			1967 Alpine	Makinen	Retired
			1969 Circuit of Ireland	Hopkirk	2nd
			Sold to W. Cresdee		
HJB 656D	April 1966	K.A2S4 821305 9F.SA.Y 40412	1966 Acropolis	Makinen	10th
			1966 Polish	Makinen	2nd
			1966 Munich–Vienna–Budapest	Makinen	1st
			1967 Monte Carlo	Lampinen	15th
			1967 East African Safari	Aaltonen	Retired
			Sold to Bembros Motors, Nairobi		
JBL 172D	April 1966	C.A2S7 821287 9F.SA.Y 40617	1966 Acropolis	Aaltonen	Retired
			1966 German	Fall	Retired
			1967 Alpine	Aaltonen	Retired
			1967 Tour de Corse	Aaltonen	Retired
			Sold to M. Wood		
JBL 494D	May 1966	C.A2S7 851190 9F.SA.Y 41279	1966 Czech	Aaltonen	1st
			1966 1000 Lakes	Lusenius	6th
			1966 Munich–Vienna–Budapest	Fall	Retired
			1966 RAC	Kallstrom	2nd
			Sold to A. Boyd		
JBL 495D	May 1966	C.A2S7 851189 9F.SA.Y 41212	1966 German	Hopkirk	Retired
			1966 London	Hopkirk	Retired
			1966 Alpine	Aaltonen	3rd
			1966 RAC	Lampinen	Crashed
			1967 Swedish	Aaltonen	3rd
			Written off		
JBL 493D	June 1966	K.A2S4 851272 9F.SA.Y 41301	1966 Czech	Makinen	3rd
			1966 1000 Lakes	Makinen	1st
			Sold to T. Makinen		

Registration number	Registered	Chassis no. / Engine no.	Events	Driver	Result
JMO 969D	July 1966	M.A2S4 850926 9F.SA.Y 40958	1966 Alpine 1966 R A C 1967 Swedish 1968 Circuit of Ireland 1968 Scottish Sold to R. Lawrence	Makinen Hopkirk Makinen Hopkirk Ytterbring	Retired Retired Retired Retired 2nd
LBL 666D	December 1966	C.A2S7 956254 9F.SA.Y 43696	1967 Monte Carlo Sold to D. Wooding	Hopkirk	6th
LBL 6D	December 1966	K.A2S4 956652	1967 Monte Carlo Retained as display car	Aaltonen	1st
LBL 606D	December 1966	C.A2S7 956238	1967 Monte Carlo 1968 T A P Sold to J. Whitehouse	Fall Hopkirk	10th 2nd
LBL 66D	December 1966		1967 Monte Carlo 1968 Tulip 1969 Silverstone 1969 Crystal Palace 1969 Mallory Park 1969 Silverstone 1969 Oulton Park 1969 Brands Hatch 1969 Salzburg Sold to L. Lambourne	Makinen Makinen Rhodes Rhodes Rhodes Rhodes Rhodes Rhodes Rhodes	41st 41st 6th 4th 4th 8th 12th 10th 1st
LBL 590E	January 1967	C.A2S7 956239 9F.SA.Y 43789	1967 Rally of the Flowers Sold to D. Friswell	Hopkirk	2nd

Reg.	Date	Chassis No.	Event	Driver	Result
LRX 827E	March 1967	KAS4 956685	1967 Tulip	Makinen	2nd
			1967 Criterium	Vernaeve	2nd
			1967 Alpine	Hopkirk	1st
			1969 Silverstone	Handley	10th
			1969 Thruxton	Handley	9th
			1969 Silverstone	Handley	7th
			1969 Crystal Palace	Handley	3rd
			1969 Mallory Park	Handley	Retired
			1969 Silverstone	Handley	10th
			1969 Brands Hatch	Handley	Retired
			1969 Salzburg	Handley	2nd
			Sold to C. Baigent		
LRX 828E	March 1967	C.A2S7 956612 / 9F.SA.Y 44521	1967 Acropolis	Aaltonen	Retired
			1967 Danube	Aaltonen	Disqualified
			Sold to BMC Australia		
LRX 829E	March 1967	K.A2S4 956691 / 9F.SA.Y 44695	1967 Tulip	Aaltonen	3rd
			1967 Geneva	Fall	1st
			Sold to BMC Australia		
LRX 830E	March 1967	C.A2S7 956615 / 9F.SA.Y 4455	1967 Acropolis	Hopkirk	1st
			1967 84 Hour Marathon	Poole/Enever/Baker	Retired
			Sold to R. McCartney		
ORX 7F	January 1968	K.2S6 1068931A	1968 Monte Carlo	Aaltonen	3rd
			Sold to W. Andrews & Co., Belfast		
ORX 77F	January 1968	K.A2S6 1068932A / 9F.SA.Y 47690	1968 Monte Carlo	Makinen	55th
			1968 Rally of the Flowers	Aaltonen	Retired
			Sold to J. Grundy		
ORX 777F	January 1968	C.A2SB 1068930A / 9F.SA.Y 47693	1968 Monte Carlo	Hopkirk	5th
			1968 Rally of the Flowers	Fall	Retired
			Sold to A. Poole		

Registration number	Registered	Chassis no. Engine no.	Events	Driver	Result
ORX 707F	January 1968	C.A2SB 1088682A 9F.SA.Y 47762	1968 Monte Carlo 1968 Tulip Sold to M. Wood	Fall Vernaeve	4th 3rd
OBL 45F	January 1968		1969 Tour de France 1969 Brands Hatch Sold to N. Higgins	Hopkirk Rhodes	14th Crashed
OBL 46F	January 1968	C.A2S7 1012035A	1968 Circuit of Ireland 1969 Brands Sold to P. Cooper	Ytterbring Handley	Retired Crashed
RBL 450F	January 1968	K.AS6 1116736A	1968 Acropolis 1969 Brands Hatch Six Hours 1969 Nurburgring Six Hours 1969 Spa 24 Hours Sold to J. Whitehouse	Aaltonen Handley/Enever Handley/Enever Handley/Enever	5th 4th Retired Retired
RJB 327F	January 1968	K.AS6 1116764A	1969 Oulton Park 1970 Southern Cross Sold to BMC Australia	Handley Culcheth	15th Retired
URX 550G	May 1969		1969 Tour de France 1969 Hockenheim Sold to B. Culcheth	Culcheth Handley	2nd class 5th class
URX 560G	May 1969	K.A2S6 1289173A 9F.XEY 53068	1969 Tour de France 1969 Hockenheim Sold to P. Browning	Handley Rhodes	Crashed 6th
XJB 308H	January 1970	XA2S2 34034A	1970 World Cup 1970 Scottish	Handley Hopkirk	Retired 2nd
YMO 881H	January 1970	XADL 131159A	1970 Southern Cross Sold to BMC Australia	Cowan	Retired
SOH 878H	January 1970	XAD2 405A	1970 84 Hour Marathon Sold to J. Handley	Handley/Poole	Retired

194

APPENDIX III—
MINI-COOPER 'S' HOMOLOGATION FORM

Form of recognition in accordance with Appendix J to the International Sporting Code of the Federation Internationale de l'Automobile for the Mini-Cooper 'S'.

FIA Recognition No. 5028
Group 1 Series Production Touring

Manufacturer: British Motor Corporation
Model: Austin/Morris Mini-Cooper 'S'
Cylinder capacity: 1275 cm³, 77·9 in³
Serial No. of chassis/body: K/A2S4 and C/A2S7
Manufacturer: British Motor Corporation
Serial No. of engine: F-SA-Y
Manufacturer: British Motor Corporation
Recognition is valid from 1st January 1966. The manufacturing of the model described in this recognition form started on 7th December 1964 and the minimum production of 5,000 identical cars, in accordance with the specifications of this form, was reached on 3rd December 1965.

Capacities and dimensions

Wheelbase: 2036·0 mm, 80·15 in
Front track: +, 6·35 mm (0·25 in) 1222·4 mm, 48·125 in
Rear track: +, 6·35 mm (0·25 in) 1176·0 mm, 46·31 in
Overall length of the car: 305·5 cm, 120·25 in
Overall width of the car: 141·0 cm, 55·5 in
Overall height of the car: 135·0 cm, 53·0 in
Capacity of fuel tank (reserve included):
    Group 1 25·0 ltrs, 5·5 gall, Imp
    Group 2 50·0 ltrs, 11·0 gall, Imp
Seating capacity: four
Weight. Total weight of car with normal equipment, water, oil, and spare wheel but without fuel or repair tools:
    651·0 kg, 1435·0 lb

Chassis and Coachwork

Chassis/body construction: unitary construction
Unitary construction, material(s): all steel
Separate construction, material(s) of chassis: all steel
Material(s) of coachwork: all steel
Number of doors: 2. Material(s): all steel
Material(s) of bonnet: steel
Material(s) of boot lid: steel
Material(s) of rear-window: safety glass
Material(s) of windscreen: toughened or laminated glass

Material(s) of front-door windows: safety glass
Material(s) of rear-door windows: safety glass
Sliding system of door windows: horizontal channels
Material(s) of rear-quarter light: safety glass

Accessories and upholstery

Interior heating: yes
Air conditioning: no
Ventilation: yes
Front seats, type of seat and upholstery: leathercloth
Weight of front seat(s), complete with supports and rails, out of car:
   7·27 kg, 16·0 lb each
Rear seats, type of seat and upholstery: leathercloth
Front bumper, material(s): steel. Weight 2·15 kg, 4·75 lb
Rear bumper, material(s): steel. Weight 2·15 kg, 4·75 lb

Wheels

Type: pressed steel
Weight (per wheel, without tyre). 3·52 kg, 7·75 lb
Method of attachment: four studs
Rim diameter: 254·0 mm, 10·0 in. Rim width: 88·9 mm, 3·5 in

Steering

Type: rack and pinion
Servo-assistance: no
Number of turns of steering wheel from lock to lock: 2·33

Suspension

Front suspension type: independent
Type of spring: hydrolastic displacer unit
Stabilizer (if fitted): none
Number of shock absorbers: 2
Type: incorporated in displacer unit
Rear suspension type: independent
Type of spring: hydrolastic displacer unit
Stabilizer (if fitted): none
Number of shock absorbers: 2
Type: incorporated in displacer unit

Brakes

Method of operation: hydraulic
Servo-assistance (if fitted), type: diaphragm servo
Number of hydraulic master cylinders: 1
Number of cylinders per wheel: 2 front, 1 rear
Bore of wheel cylinder(s): front 44·45 mm, 1·75 in
                    rear 15·875 mm, 0·625 in

Drum brakes

Inside diameter: 177·8 mm 7·0 in
Length of brake linings: 171·5 mm 6·75 in
Width of brake linings: 31·75 mm 1·25 in
Number of shoes per brake: 2
Total area per brake: 10887·0 mm², 16·8 in²

Disc brakes

Outside diameter: 190·5 mm, 7·5 in
Thickness of disc: 9·52 mm, 0·375 in
Length of brake linings: approx 69·85 mm, 2·75 in
Width of brake linings: approx 42·85 mm, 1·68 in
Number of pads per brake: 2
Total area per brake: 5575·0 mm², 8·64 in²

Engine

Cycle: 4 stroke
Number of cylinders: 4
Cylinder arrangement: in line
Bore: 70·63 mm, 2·78 in
Stroke: 21–33 mm, 3·2 in
Capacity per cylinder: 318·7 cm³, 19·4 in³
Total cylinder capacity: 1275 cm³, 77·9 in³
Material(s) of cylinder block: cast iron
Material(s) of sleeves (if fitted): cast iron
Cylinder head, material(s): cast iron
Number fitted: 1
Number of inlet ports: 2
Number of exhaust ports: 3
Compression ratio: 9·75 to 1
Volume of one combustion chamber: 21·4 cm³, 1·306 in³
Piston, material: aluminium alloy
Number of rings: 4
Distance from gudgeon pin centre line to highest point of piston crown:
    37·91/38·03 mm, 1·492/1·497 in
Crankshaft: stamped
Type of crankshaft: integral
Number of crankshaft main bearings: 3
Material of bearing cap: sg iron
System of lubrication: oil in sump
Capacity, lubricant: 5·11 ltrs, 9 pts
Oil cooler: yes
Method of engine cooling: pressurized water
Capacity of cooling system: 2·981 ltrs, 5·25 pts
Cooling fan (if fitted) diameter: 26·51 cm, 10·44 in
Number of blades of cooling fan: 16

Bearings

Crankshaft main, type: thin wall, dia 50·82 mm, 2·00 in
Connecting rod big end, type: thin wall, dia 41·29 mm, 1·69 in

Weights

Flywheel (clean): 7·36 kg, 16·25 lb
Flywheel with clutch (all turning parts): 11·89 kg, 26·25 lb
Crankshaft: 11·43 kg, 25·25 lb
Connecting rod: 0·68 kg, 1·50 lb
Piston with rings and pin: 0·354 kg, 0·78 lb

Four stroke engines

Number of camshafts: 1
Location: cylinder block
Type of camshaft drive: duplex chain
Type of valve operation: ohv pushrod and rocker

Inlet

Material(s) of inlet manifold: aluminium alloy
Diameter of valves: 35·59/35·71 mm, 1·401/1·406 in
Max. valve lift: 7·62 mm, 0·300 in
Number of valve springs: 2 per valve
Type of spring: coil
Number of valves per cylinder: 1
Tappet clearance for checking timing (cold): 0·53 mm, 0·021 in
Valves open at (with tolerance for tappet clearance indicated): 10° BTDC
Valves close at (with tolerance for tappet clearance indicated): 50° ATDC
Air filter type: replaceable paper element

Exhaust

Material(s) of exhaust manifold: steel pressing
Diameter of valves: 30·86/30·96 mm 1·214/1·219 in
Max. valve lift: 8·10 mm, 0·318 in
Number of valve springs: 2 per valve
Type of spring: coil
Number of valves per cylinder: 1
Tappet clearance for checking timing (cold): 0·53 mm, 0·021 in
Valves open at (with tolerance for tappet clearance indicated): 51° BBDC
Valves close at (with tolerance for tappet clearance indicated): 21° ABDC

Carburation

Number of carburetters fitted: 2
Type: variable choke
Make: SU
Model: HS2
Number of mixture passages per carburetter: 1

Flange hole diameter of exit port(s) of carburetter: 31·75 mm
Minimum diameter of venturi/minimum diameter with piston at maximum
  height (example: SU) 23·01 mm, 0·906 in

Engine accessories
Fuel pump: electrical
No. fitted: 1
Type of ignition system: HT coil
No. of distributors: 1
No. of ignition coils: 1
No. of spark plugs per cylinder: 1
Generator type: dynamo/alternator – number fitted: 1
Method of drive: wedge belt
Voltage of generator: 12 volts
Battery, number: 1
Location: luggage compartment
Voltage of battery: 12 volts

Engine and car performances (as declared by manufacturer in catalogue)
Max. engine output: 75 (type of horsepower: BHP) at 5,800 rev/min
Max. torque: 80 at 3,000 rev/min
Max. speed of the car. 152·9 km/h 95·0 mile/h

Camshaft dimensions
Inlet cam
Centre of camshaft to tip of lobe: 20·37 mm, 0·802 in
Centre of camshaft to radius of bearing: 13·97 mm, 0·550 in
Diameter of bearing: 26·17 mm, 1·109 in
Exhaust cam
Centre of camshaft to tip of lobe: 20·55 mm, 0·809 in
Centre of camshaft to radius of bearing: 13·79 mm, 0·543 in
Diameter of bearing: 27·69 mm, 1·09 in

Clutch
Type of clutch: diaphragm spring
No. of plates: 1
Diameter of clutch plates: 18·1 cm, 7·125 in
Diameter of linings, inside: 13·34 cm, 5·25 in
                    outside: 18·1 cm, 7·125 in
Method of operating clutch: hydraulic

Gearbox
Manual type, make: B M C
No. of gearbox ratios forward: 4.
Sychronized forward ratios: 3
Location of gear-shift: remote control central floor lever

Gear ratios

1st gear ratio: 3·2   no. of teeth: 26/30 × 32/13
2nd gear ratio: 1·916 no. of teeth: 26/20 × 28/19
3rd gear ratio: 1·357 no. of teeth: 26/20 × 24/23
4th gear ratio: 1·0:1
Reverse ratio: 3·2   no. of teeth: 26/20 × 18/32 × 32/18

Gear ratios (alternative)

1st gear ratio: 2·57   no. of teeth: 23/22 × 32/13
2nd gear ratio: 1·72   no. of teeth: 23/22 × 28/17
3rd gear ratio: 1·25   no. of teeth: 23/22 × 24/20
4th gear ratio: 1·0:1
Reverse ratio: 2·57   no. of teeth: 23/22 × 18/13 × 32/18

Final drive

Type of final drive: helical spur gear
Type of differential: bevel pinion
Final drive ratio: 3·44:1
Number of teeth: 62/18

Amendments

The vehicle described in this form has been subject to the following amendments:

Final drive ratio: 4·133:1
Number of teeth: 15/62
Alternative heavy duty export suspension. Hydrolastic displacer unit part numbers C–21A 1819 and 1821
Front track: 49·125 in, 1247·8 mm
Rear track: 47·31 in, 1201·4 mm
Fuel tank: 60 litres, 13.21 galls
Road wheel: weight 4·65 kg, 10·23 lb
Rim width: 114·3 mm, 4·5 in
Flywheel (steel): 5·03 kg 11·06 lb
Exhaust manifold: C–AEG 365
Limited slip differential: C–AJJ 3303
Final drive ratio: 3·765:1, 3·938:1, 4·26:1, 4·788:1 4·35:1
Number of teeth: 17/64, 16/63, 16/64, 14/67, 15/65
Sump guard: C–AJJ 3320 (21A 1675, 22A 437)
Inlet cam: diameter of bearing 28·17 mm
Fuel tank capacity: 50 litres 11.0 gall, Imp (Group 1)
Magnesium alloy wheel: part number 21A 1968 (Group 2)
Weight: 2·31 kg, 5·094 lb
Fixing: four studs and nuts
Diameter: 254·0 mm, 10·0 in
Width: 114·3 mm, 4·5 in

Peg drive conversion kit: C–AJJ 3338 (Group 2) to be used in conjunction with magnesium alloy wheel part number 21A 1968

Track dimensions with this conversion are: front 49·75 in, 1264·0 mm; rear 47·93 in, 1217·4 mm ($\pm$, 0·25 in, 6·35 mm)

Wing extension kit: C–AJJ 3353

Magnesium alloy wheel: part number 21A 2132 (Group 2)

Weight: 2·84 kg, 6·25 lb

Fixing: four studs and nuts

Diameter: 254·0 mm, 10·0 in

Width: 139·7 mm, 5·5 in

Track front: 1285·24 mm, 50·62 in ($\pm$ 6·35 mm, 0·25 in)

Track rear: 1240·30 mm 48·85 in ($\pm$ 6·35 mm, 0·25 in)

Inlet manifold: (material) aluminium alloy (evolution)

Wing extension kit: part number C–AJJ 3316 (Group 2)

Supplementary front shock absorber kit: part number C–AJJ 3362 (Group 2)

Front suspension adjustable tie rod: part number 21A 1092 (Group 2)

Rear suspension heavy duty bump rubber kit: part number C–AJJ 3313 (Group 2)

Crankshaft locking plate: part number C–AHT 146 (Group 2)

Steering column rake adjusting bracket: part number AHT–164 (Group 2)

Heavy duty gearbox mounting kit: part number C–AJJ 3366 (Group 2)

Modified rocker shaft: part number AEG 399 at engine number 9F–SA–Y 48058 (evolution)

Perspex window set for rear-window, front-window and rear-quarter windows: part number C–AJJ 3363 (Group 2)

Suspension arms lower wishbone set: part number C–AJJ 3364 (Group 2)

Thermostat blanking insert: part number 11G 176 (Group 2)

Four-speed synchromesh gearbox introduced at engine number 9F–XE–Y (evolution Group 1)

Steel road wheel (Group 2)

Weight: 477 kg, 10·5 lb

Fixing: four studs and nuts

Diameter: 304·8 mm, 12·0 in

Width: 114·4 mm, 4·5 in

Front track: 1268·5 mm, 49·94 in

Rear track: 1225·0 mm, 48·19 in

Aluminium alloy doors; part number C–AJJ 3379 (Group 2)

Aluminium bonnet and boot lid: part number C–AJJ 3380

Magnesium alloy road wheels: part numbers C–AHT 248 and 249 (Group 2)

Weight: 4·08 kg, 9·0 lb

Fixing: four studs and nuts

Diameter: 304·8 mm, 12·0 in

Widths: 117·8 mm, 7·0 in and 152·4 mm, 6·0 in

Front track: 1284·0 mm, 50·56 in and 1291·0 mm, 50·81 in

Rear track: 1250·9 mm, 49·25 in

Plastic cooling fan 11 blades: part number 12G 1305 (evolution)

Diameter: 26·51 cm, 10·44 in

Eight-port cylinder head: part number C–AEG 612 (Group 2)

Material: cast iron
Number of inlet ports: four
Number of exhaust ports: four
Inlet valve diameter: 35·6 mm, 1·40 in
Exhaust valve diameter: 29·3 mm, 1·15 in
Cylinder head: part number 12G 938 introduced at engine number 9F–XE–Y
    54437 (evolution)
Diameter of exhaust valve: 29·21 mm, 1·15 in
Rubber cone spring suspension (Group 2)
Number of shock absorbers: two
Type: hydraulic telescopic
Type of spring: rubber cone
Aluminium alloy eight-port cylinder head: part number C–AHT 346 (Group 2)
Number of inlet ports: four
Number of exhaust ports: four
Inlet valve diameter: 35·6 mm, 1·40 in
Exhaust valve diameter: 29·3 mm, 1·15 in

INDEX